Murder Most Vile
Volume 23
18 Truly Shocking
Murder Cases

Robert Keller

Please Leave Your Review of This Book At
http://bit.ly/kellerbooks

ISBN-13: 9781728751740

© 2018 by Robert Keller

robertkellerauthor.com

Table of Contents

Deadly Intent

Misty Witherspoon should never have married a police officer. With her shopping obsession, a millionaire businessman might have been a better match, one with very deep pockets and an extremely generous nature. Still, Misty was young and she was in love. She didn't think twice when Quinn Witherspoon asked for her hand in marriage. Quinn was a K-9 officer with the Concord Police Department. He loved his job and he was good at it. That part, Misty got. What she didn't get was that law enforcement jobs are generally not that well paid.

Fast forward eleven years and we find Quinn and Misty living an apparently happy life in Mooresville, North Carolina. There were three children in the picture by now, making them a handsome family unit. Quinn was still with the police department and also actively involved in the running of the Whitman Park Baptist Church, which he served as a deacon and also as church treasurer. Misty was a good mom and was devoted to her children.

Scratch below the surface, though, and a different picture emerges. The couple was drowning in debt, much of it as a result of Misty's reckless spending. She simply did not appreciate that the family was required to work within a budget, and her constantly maxed-out credit cards were a frequent source of friction between her and her husband. Quinn was generally a patient man, but his wife's behavior often left him exasperated. In all other respects, Misty was a responsible adult. When it came to money, though, she was like a kid in a candy store or, more aptly, a junkie looking for her next fix.

Quinn, however, did not know the half of it. That would come to light in 2004 when his pastor called him in to tell him that $18,000 was missing from the church's bank account. It did not take a forensic audit to discover who was responsible. Misty had been siphoning off money that had been entrusted to her husband's care. And she'd hardly been subtle about it. Confronted with the evidence, Misty tearfully confessed. She'd taken the money, she said, to settle arrear utility bills. It was either that or leave her children without water and electricity. The money Quinn had given her to pay the family's expenses had been squandered on luxuries.

Fortunately for Misty, the church elders decided not to press charges. An agreement was struck whereby Quinn would repay the money, and the matter was put to bed. But Quinn had only uncovered the tip of the iceberg. What he didn't know was that his wife was also juggling mortgage payments, had maxed out several credit cards he wasn't even aware of, had fraudulently acquired several more credit cards in her sister's name, and was fielding numerous calls each day from irate creditors.

Those details would only be brought to his attention in March 2005, when Quinn went to his credit union to discuss a delinquent account and learned the full extent of his wife's duplicity. Thereafter, he significantly reduced the spending limit on his credit card and canceled the linked facility that had been issued to Misty. He also signed off on a payment plan for the settlement of the delinquent accounts, which meant that the family had to tighten their already strained belts. Some harsh words were exchanged that night, and the gist of it was that Misty really had to start acting responsibly with money.

Quinn Witherspoon appears to have been a particularly trusting individual. Despite all evidence to the contrary, he continued to believe his wife when she said that she would mend her ways. Misty retained responsibility for paying the family's bills, and it wasn't long before she was back to her old habits. Utilities and mortgage again went unpaid as she diverted the money to fund her spending. Her level of duplicity was such that when she and Quinn were at home together, she'd carry the phone around with her so that she could field any calls that came in. Inevitably, those calls would be from some or other company, demanding payment of an arrear bill.

But of course, this was a deception that could only be maintained for so long. On September 6, 2005, Misty received a letter of demand from Duke Power saying that her electricity would be cut off unless settlement of the arrears was made within seven days. Misty did nothing about that letter until the afternoon of September 13. Then she called Duke Power and asked for an extension on the heavily overdue account. Since the grace period had already expired, they gave her just 24 hours to come up with the money.

Misty was now in a spot. She had no way to pay the debt which meant that she was going to have to confess to Quinn that she had again deceived him. After stealing money from the church, after defrauding her sister, after running her family close to financial ruin, after all the promises she'd made the last time around, she had fallen off the wagon again. Quinn was a patient man, but even he had his limits. She did not know how he'd react.

And so Misty Witherspoon made a decision, a terrible, wicked decision that would end up costing an innocent man his life and leaving three innocent children to be raised without either of their parents. Misty decided that she'd rather kill her husband than admit to him that she had let him down again.

At around 2:08 p.m. on September 13, 2005, a dispatcher at the Iredell County 911 call center received a call from an apparently distraught Misty Witherspoon. She said that she had been bringing her husband his service pistol when she had tripped and accidentally fired the weapon. Quinn had been hit in the head and she believed that he had been killed.

The shooting of one of their own sent police officers racing to the Witherspoon residence. First to arrive was Officer Corey Barnette, who found Quinn lying face down on a couch, his pistol on the floor a few feet away beside a hard-covered children's book. According to Misty, she had been carrying the gun when she'd stepped on the book, causing her foot to slide. That is what had caused the gun to fire.

By now, an ambulance had arrived, and it did not take the EMTs long to confirm what Officer Barnette already knew. Quinn Witherspoon was dead. In fact, as Barnette had already noted and as one of the medics now pointed out, the blood around the bullet wound had already dried. That suggested that Misty Witherspoon had not called 911 immediately after the shooting. It was the first indication that she was not telling the truth.

Over the next 24 hours, Misty would repeat her story, almost verbatim, to several other officers. But nothing that she said added up. The position of the body, the angle of the bullet wound and the location of the single shell casing all suggested that someone had leaned over Quinn Witherspoon and shot him as he dozed. In order to resolve the inconsistencies, detectives asked Misty to do a re-enactment of the shooting. Then they asked to make another statement, clearing up any earlier discrepancies; then they brought her in for a second interview and then a third.

Misty had spent most of her adult life around cops, and she must have known by now that the police were not convinced by her story. And so, during an interview on October 5, she changed it. She now said that the reason she'd been carrying her husband's gun that day was because she had decided to kill herself.

According to this latest version of events, Misty said that she had spoken to the power company at around 1:30 and had been told that her electricity was about to be cut off. That had left her feeling distraught, so she had walked to the bathroom to "think things through." There, she'd opened a closet to look for some hand lotion. As she did so, her husband's gun fell out. She took this as a "sign."

Picking up the gun, Misty had walked with it to the outside workshop, where she planned on shooting herself. She would have done it, too, had Quinn's K-9 dog, Tank, not come in and started nudging her. The dog appeared to know what she was about to do, and it seemed like he was preventing her from doing it.

Misty then walked back into the house, still carrying the gun. She was trembling so badly over her near-suicide that she thought she might collapse. She therefore grabbed the backrest of the couch where Quinn was sleeping, holding onto it to steady herself. Then one of the family cats jumped up onto the backrest and bumped against her arm. That was what caused her to pull the trigger.

If anything, this new story was less believable than the first. The police certainly weren't buying it. That same day, Misty Witherspoon was arrested and charged with first-degree murder. Further charges followed, for identity theft, for obtaining property by false pretenses, and for embezzlement. Misty struck a plea deal and admitted to those. She remained adamant, however, that her husband's death had been an accident.

Misty was still telling that story when the matter came to trial in June 2007. However, the evidence soon stacked up against her. Particularly damning was the medical examiner's report, stating that Quinn Witherspoon had been shot from a distance of no more than six inches. Then there was a courtroom re-enactment, using a mannequin, which showed that the trajectory of the bullet that had killed Quinn made Misty's version of events impossible. She could not have been standing where she said she was when the bullet was fired.

The defense, of course, produced its own expert witness who contradicted the prosecution evidence, but in the end, the jury was not convinced. Misty Witherspoon was found guilty as charged and was sentenced to life in prison without the possibility of parole.

The killing of Quinn Witherspoon must rank as one of the most senseless murders of all time. Quinn was a devoted father and a dedicated police officer who also appears to have had an inordinate amount of patience with his wayward wife. Time and again, she let him down, and time and again, he forgave her. Is it that much of a stretch to think that he might not have done so again after her latest infraction? Instead, Misty decided on an extreme solution to her problems. According to a clinical psychologist who testified at the trial, Misty was suffering from depression, anxiety, and stress at the time of the shooting and thus could not form the "specific intent to kill." Nonetheless, she did form that intent, she did pull the trigger, she did end the life of a good man. It is only fitting that she forfeits her freedom in recompense. This is one bill that Misty Witherspoon will not be able to dodge.

Love Kills

Marc Van Beers could hardly believe his luck. The nerdy, 36-year-old tax accountant had signed up to a dating service, expecting to be paired with someone homely, someone who, like him, was having trouble finding a mate. He had not anticipated a petite, blond beauty like Aurore Martin. Aurore was more than just beautiful, she was sophisticated, educated and charming. On their very first meeting, Marc was smitten. Over their next few dates he was both stunned and delighted to find that Aurore was attracted to him, too. When he popped the question just a few months into their relationship in 1995, she immediately said yes.

And so Marc and Aurore were wed, tying the knot in Marc's home town of Brussels, Belgium. Thereafter, the newlyweds departed for a honeymoon on the beautiful Mediterranean island of Corsica. For Marc, who had all but resigned himself to the lonely life of a bachelor, it must have seemed like a dream come true. All too soon, that dream would be transformed into a nightmare.

On the evening of May 10, 1995, a couple of American tourists were returning to their hotel after a day spent basking on a beautiful Corsican beach. It was dark by now, and the road was narrow and winding with a steep drop-off to one side. Sensibly, the driver was maintaining a low speed. Then suddenly, a woman staggered into the road ahead, a young woman with blond hair, wearing a blood-spattered summer dress. The driver of the vehicle immediately stopped, and she and her passenger scrambled out to help the injured woman.

But the woman didn't seem to want their help. She was crying hysterically, pointing into the darkness, babbling in French. From what the would-be rescuers could determine, she was saying that her car had swerved off the road and fallen over the cliff with her husband still inside. If that was the case, the tourists realized, there was very little chance that he had survived. They suggested driving to the hotel to get help, but the sobbing woman refused to leave so one of them stayed with her while the other went to summon the authorities.

Police and emergency services were soon on the scene, with paramedics quickly examining the woman, determining that she had no major injuries and then sedating her and transporting her to the local hospital. Then rescuers fixed lines and abseiled down to the stricken vehicle lodged in the ravine below. The driver was still in his seat, still restrained by his seatbelt. But it was immediately clear that he was beyond help. He'd suffered severe head trauma in the accident.

Meanwhile, at the hospital, the female accident victim had been treated for minor bruises and abrasions and was finally ready to talk to the police. Sobbing inconsolably, she identified herself as Aurore Van Beers and the driver of the vehicle as her husband, Marc. She explained that they were on honeymoon and that they had decided to go for a moonlight drive in the cabriolet that they were renting. All had been fine until a dog had run into the road and Marc had swerved to avoid it, losing control of the vehicle in the process. As the car had plowed through the brush on its path towards the precipice, Marc had shouted for her to jump, which she'd done immediately. She'd barely hit the ground when there was a loud crash from below. She'd then climbed back up to the road to summon help.

The Corsican authorities had no reason to doubt the story. Neither did they spend much time on a forensic examination. They simply declared Marc Van Beers death an accident and authorized the release of his body for transport back to Belgium. There, the widow Van Beers was united in grief with her new in-laws as they discussed the funeral arrangements. It was these discussions that triggered the first feelings of unease amongst Marc's relatives.

According to Aurore, Marc had spoken at length of his desire to be cremated. Marc's parents found this strange, since the family had a plot at a local cemetery where generations of Van Beers had been interred. It had always been tacitly agreed that the family tradition would continue, and Marc had never suggested otherwise to his parents. Aurore was nonetheless adamant that he had shared that wish with her. The elder Van Beers had to be quite forceful to overrule her.

And then there was the issue of the insurance policies. There were seven of these in total, with an accumulated value of $1.3 million. No one was in any way surprised that Aurore was the beneficiary of these instruments. But seven policies? Many of them recent, and the latest carrying a double indemnity clause for accidental death? Coupled with

Aurore's vociferous arguments for cremation, it raised suspicion. So much so that Marc's family approached the Belgian authorities and demanded an investigation.

But although an inquiry was launched, it was cursory at best. The Belgian police simply interviewed Aurore, read through the Corsican case files, and then declared that Marc's death had indeed been a tragic accident. Aurore was left to cash her insurance policies and get on with her life. If she had murdered her husband for money, as the Van Beers family suspected, then she'd gotten away with it.

Around one year after the accident, Marc's uncle was reading a magazine when a particular article made him sit up and take notice. The story was about a young woman named Ursula Deschamps who had died in a tragic accident shortly after her marriage to a German national named Peter Uwe Schmidt. What was really striking about the story were the similarities to the Van Beers case. The couple had been driving along a road at night when Schmidt lost control of their car and drove it into a canal. He had managed to escape and swim to safety while his young wife had gone to the depths with the vehicle and had drowned. At the subsequent inquiry, Schmidt had pled guilty to involuntary homicide and had received three years' probation. That ruling had not prevented him from cashing a policy worth nearly $800,000 on his wife's life.

The similarities between the cases were intriguing. And while the Belgian police were not entirely convinced that they were connected, they agreed to question Peter Schmidt in order to determine whether there was any link between him and Aurore Martin. The problem was that Schmidt proved a difficult man to find. All that the police were able to determine was that he was a former army officer who was suspected of involvement in various insurance scams.

Unable to track down Schmidt, detectives turned their attention back to Aurore. From a former friend, they learned that much of what Aurore had told Marc and his family was a lie. Aurore had claimed that she was from a wealthy family, that she was university educated and that she was an aspiring actress. In truth, she'd grown up in poverty, was a high school dropout and had worked as a prostitute before meeting Marc Van Beers.

Lying about your past isn't a crime, of course, but it did set alarm bells jangling. And those alarms were ringing even louder when the police interviewed Aurore again. She was less co-operative this time, although she did reaffirm the lies about her background. She also denied knowing anyone named Peter Schmidt. The police didn't believe her. In fact, they were so unconvinced by her performance that they decided to reopen the investigation into Marc Van Beers's death.

Van Beers's body was exhumed and an autopsy determined that the injuries he'd sustained could not have been caused by a road accident. Instead, it appeared that he'd been beaten to death, his brain pulped with some sort of club, possibly a baseball bat. Additionally, pathologists determined that the scratches and abrasions Marc had received in the car crash were postmortem, meaning that he was already dead by the time his vehicle went over the cliff.

An arrest warrant was now issued for Aurore. By the time the police arrived at her apartment, however, they found that she had already

fled. Then came another snippet of information. Investigators found
that Aurore had lied about not knowing Peter Schmidt. They had, in
fact, met years earlier while attending a rock climbing course. The
question was, were they now on the run together? The police thought
that they were and decided to go public in their hunt for the fugitives.
Yet despite massive press coverage, despite even the involvement of
Interpol, Schmidt and Martin remained frustratingly at large. The
suspicion was that the might have left Europe, and that suspicion
turned out to be correct.

In October of 1997, the FBI received a tip that Schmidt and Martin
were living in Miami Beach, Florida. The fugitives were hardly
keeping a low profile, renting a lavishly appointed Collins Avenue
apartment, buying a boat and a luxury sedan, eating at the best
restaurants, enjoying the city's nightlife. But they were clever enough
to avoid using credit cards, and that made them difficult to track. They
were also skittish. After an article about their case appeared in a
popular French magazine, they fled to the Bahamas, getting out of
town just as Federal agents were closing in.

Had Schmidt and Martin remained on the run, it is unlikely that the
Feds would have tracked them down. But they had fled Miami in a
hurry, leaving behind many of their valuable possessions, including
the luxury yacht that Schmidt had just purchased. They were also
running low on cash. And so, one month after leaving Florida, the
fugitives were back and selling off their possessions at knockdown
prices.

The most valuable of their assets was their yacht "To Life" which
Schmidt quickly offloaded to a Miami businessman at around half its

market value. However, the man still owed $50,000 on the sale price, and Schmidt was pressing him for payment, even threatening to kill him. After the man alerted the FBI, agents were able to trace those threatening calls to a public phone near Miami International Airport, and it was there that they nabbed Peter Schmidt. Aurore was taken into custody the following day.

Schmidt and Martin were extradited to Belgium in 1998, but it would take three years before they were eventually brought to trial. By then, Aurore had already given the police a confession to Marc Van Beers's murder, fingering Schmidt as the mastermind and casting herself in the role of reluctant participant. She said that she and Schmidt had been lovers before she met Van Beers. Schmidt had confided in her that he'd killed his wife for her life insurance, and the two had then plotted a similar murder. Shortly after, Martin had listed with a matrimonial agency and been hooked up with Marc Van Beers.

As for the murder itself, Aurore said that she had convinced Marc to go for a drive, as instructed by Schmidt. At a predetermined spot, she had complained of feeling nauseous and had asked Marc to pull over. She then got out of the car, knelt at the roadside and pretended to throw up. As Marc tried to comfort her, another car pulled up behind them and two men got out. These were the men hired by Schmidt to carry out the actual murder. They beat Marc to death at the side of the road, while Aurore remained kneeling, covering her ears in a vain attempt to drown out her husband's pleas. His final words were, "Please don't hurt my wife."

Peter Schmidt and Aurore Martin were both convicted of murder. The sentences, however, were a bitter disappointment to the Van Beers family. They had hoped that the evil couple would be put away for life. Instead, Aurore got just fifteen years, Schmidt just twenty. Even worse, the killers would serve only a portion of their sentences. Aurore was released in 2007, having served just five years; Peter Schmidt walked free a year later after only six years behind bars.

By all accounts, the "Diabolical Lovers" (as they were dubbed in the Belgian press) are back together again, whereabouts unknown. Who knows what evil plans they are hatching now.

And Never Let Her Go

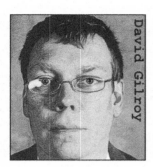

Office romances can be dangerous things. First there is the risk of discovery, the potential damage to reputation, the possibility of losing one's job. Then there is the problem of breakups, the awkwardness of having to face one's former paramour day by day, long after the flames of passion have died out. This is made doubly difficult when one of the lovers is ready to move on while the other refuses to accept that it's over.

Take David Gilroy and Suzanne Pilley, for example. David was a married father of two, employed as a junior executive by Infrastructure Managers Ltd, an accounting firm based in Edinburgh, Scotland; Suzanne was 38, single, and worked as a bookkeeper for the same organization. How and when they first embarked on their illicit relationship is not that relevant to this case. What is relevant is that it was Suzanne who ended it and David who refused to let go. Even after returning to his wife and kids, he continued to pester her at work and to bombard her with text messages and voicemail. There was little that Suzanne could do about this stalking. She wasn't about to quit her job just to avoid him. All she could do was to get on with her life and hope that David would eventually accept that she wasn't coming back to him.

On the morning of May 4, 2010, Suzanne Pilley followed her usual routine, taking a bus from her residence to central Edinburgh, making a phone call to her mother en route, stopping at the Sainsbury's store in St. Andrew Square to buy a few items, then following North St. David Street to her workplace on Thistle Street. It was a short walk along a busy route, one that Suzanne made daily and could have made in her sleep. On this day, however, Suzanne didn't reach her destination. She wasn't at her desk at 9 a.m., and she still hadn't shown up by midday. That was when her supervisor decided to check on her. After phoning Suzanne's cell and home number and getting no response, the supervisor dialed Suzanne's mother. Sylvia Pilley was mystified by her daughter's no-show. After all, Suzanne had been on her way to work when they'd spoken earlier that morning.

Sylvia and her younger daughter, Gail, would spend that entire afternoon phoning and texting friends and relatives, growing increasingly anxious as each reported that they had not seen Suzanne. In the meantime, Suzanne's father, Robert, went to her house and found it securely locked and Suzanne nowhere to be found. Eventually, at 6 p.m., Sylvia called the police and reported her daughter missing.

Edinburgh is a city of nearly half-a-million people, and the disappearance of an adult woman from a busy city street during the early morning rush hour seemed highly improbable. The most likely explanation was that Suzanne had gone off somewhere by herself without letting anyone know. But that possibility was quickly dismissed once detectives started talking to the missing woman's friends and family. That was simply not like Suzanne. She was close to her parents and sister and had a pet cat that she loved and would not have left unattended. She also had a new man in her life and appeared happy in the relationship. Nothing in her recent behavior suggested that she was under stress or considering any drastic moves.

Detectives heard those same sentiments when they started questioning Suzanne's work colleagues on the afternoon of May 5. "Easy going," "trustworthy," and "reliable" were the adjectives that were most frequently mentioned. "Out of character" was what they were told when they suggested that Suzanne might have decided to go off on her own. The officers also heard something else during these sessions. They heard about the relationship between Suzanne and fellow employee, David Gilroy. Questioning Gilroy would have to wait, though. He was absent from the office that day, on a business trip to Argyll, over 130 miles away.

Just before 11:30 on the night of May 4, David Gilroy arrived at Edinburgh's Corstorphine Police Station and asked to speak to the detective in charge of the Pilley investigation. He apologized for coming in so late but explained that he had just returned from his business trip. He was keen to assist the police in any way he could. Asked about his relationship with Suzanne, he readily admitted that they had been lovers, although he insisted that it had ended amicably after he'd decided to go back to his wife. He then contradicted the other witnesses police had spoken to, saying that he had noticed some erratic behavior from Suzanne in recent days. Nothing serious, he said, but she had certainly not been herself.

Gilroy had been extremely forthcoming and appeared genuinely concerned about his former lover's wellbeing. But detectives had noticed something unusual during the interview, several superficial scratches on his hands. Asked about these, Gilroy said that he'd scratched himself while trimming back some rose bushes in his garden. With no reason to believe otherwise, the detectives thanked him for his cooperation and bade him goodnight.

Over the days that followed, the Lothian and Borders Police initiated a high-profile public appeal for information about Suzanne Pilley's disappearance. This included several large, electronic billboards that were erected around the Edinburgh city center to display images and CCTV footage of the missing woman. It seemed impossible that Suzanne could have vanished without somebody noticing something unusual. And yet that was apparently what had happened. The campaign produced not a single workable lead. At the same time, the police were monitoring Suzanne's cell phone and bank account, growing increasingly concerned as neither showed any activity. On May 11, a police spokesman informed the press that they now believed that "something sinister" had happened to Suzanne Pilley. A week later, it was announced that the case was being treated as a murder inquiry.

But how do you investigate a murder when there is no body, no crime scene, and not a single witness? The answer is that you turn to technology. Over the last couple of decades, surveillance cameras have become an increasingly invasive presence in our everyday lives. This is particularly true in Great Britain which has more CCTV cameras per square mile than any other nation on earth. But despite the protestations of libertarians, these cameras have proved their worth in resolving any number of criminal cases. In the mysterious disappearance of Suzanne Pilley, they would prove invaluable.

As police experts studied the footage from various cameras along Suzanne's regular route, they began to build up a picture of the missing woman's last known movements. Suzanne was picked up by the camera inside the bus she took to work that morning; she was seen shopping inside the Sainsbury's store; she was tracked by the cameras covering St. Andrew Square and was there, captured by the lens, walking along North St. David Street. She was seen turning into Thistle Street at 8:53, but there was no camera covering this section of the route, and so the police were unable to say whether she had actually entered the building where she worked. Was it possible that Suzanne had made it inside the building and been killed there? Was it possible that the body was still concealed somewhere on the premises? In order to test this theory, investigators decided to bring in a team of cadaver dogs.

These uniquely skilled canines perform a highly specialized role in police work. They are trained to sniff out the scent of death. Released at the premises of Infrastructure Managers Ltd, the pair of dogs were given free rein of the four-story building. They reacted to two locations in particular, a small recess under the basement stairs and a parking bay in the same area – a bay reserved for David Gilroy.

This was vital evidence. It not only indicated that there had been a dead body in the parking garage, but it suggested that that body had been in the vicinity of David Gilroy's vehicle. With Gilroy now elevated to the top of the suspect list, the police began looking into his movements on the day of Suzanne's disappearance. He was picked up on CCTV, arriving at the office just after 8:30. Shortly after, he logged into his computer, but from that point on, until 9:15, the computer was idle. So where had Gilroy been during this crucial period, which just happened to coincide with the time frame during which Suzanne had disappeared. Was it possible that he was down in the basement, snuffing out the life of the woman who had rejected him?

The police couldn't say for sure, but the evidence against Gilroy would soon begin stacking up. For example, his first action on returning to his desk that morning was to schedule a visit for the following day to a client, a school in Lochgilphead, Argyll. Nothing startling about that. Gilroy managed several accounts in the area and was required to visit them as part of his duties. But he usually did so according to a roster. This visit was unscheduled and, as would later be ascertained, entirely without purpose.

And there were other aspects of Gilroy's behavior which appeared odd to investigators. Several times during the day, he was picked up on CCTV, pacing the lane outside the parking garage. He also left the office twice that day. On the first occasion, he'd gone home to fetch his car. Why do that when he'd taken the bus to the office that morning? Then, he'd visited a local supermarket and bought several cans of air freshener.

The investigators had by now built up a compelling picture of what might have happened to Suzanne Pilley. They believed that Suzanne had been confronted by David as she'd entered the building. He'd wanted to discuss the breakdown of their relationship and, rather than cause a scene, Suzanne had agreed to go with him down into the basement to talk things over. Once there, her refusal to consider a reconciliation had thrown Gilroy into a rage and he'd killed her, probably by strangulation. He'd then dragged her body into the recess, leaving it there until he could return with his car and load her into the

trunk, where she would remain overnight. The air fresheners had been
bought to conceal the odor of death from human nostrils, even if they
had proved inadequate to mask those scents from trained canines.

It was a convincing depiction of what might have happened to
Suzanne. Indeed, it was the only explanation that fit the evidence. But
one question remained. If Gilroy had killed his former lover, what had
he done with her body? This was where Gilroy's unscheduled trip to
Argyll came in.

The journey from Edinburgh to Argyll runs almost the width of
Scotland, covering rugged, mountainous territory. The easiest and
fastest route is via the Rest-and-be -Thankful Pass, and this is the route
that Gilroy had always taken in the past. On this day, however, ping-
backs from cell phone masts showed that he'd detoured north, via
Stirling and Tyndrum, turning his phone off several times during the
journey. Why had he done this? Investigators believed that he'd been
trying to hide his location, a site somewhere along the heavily forested
route where he'd stopped to bury Suzanne's body.

This theory was all but confirmed when police experts analyzed
Gilroy's travel time and fuel usage between various locations. One
stretch in particular, between Tyndrum and Inveraray, was of interest.
The distance is usually covered in around 36 minutes, but on this day it
took Gilroy two-and-a-half hours. An analysis of his fuel consumption
over this short journey, indicated that he had driven an additional 124
miles, all of it while his cell phone was turned off.

It does not take a major leap of logic to conclude that this stretch of road is where Gilroy made a detour to hide Suzanne's body. But the area is remote, vast, and covered by dense forest. Despite extensive searches, covering over 400 square miles and involving police, search and rescue specialists, civilian volunteers, sniffer dogs, infrared and other technologies, no trace of Suzanne Pilley was found.

David Gilroy might have thought that the lack of a body would get him off the hook, but he was wrong. Four murder cases in Scottish history had been successfully prosecuted without a corpse, and none of those had as much circumstantial evidence as this one. There was the narrow time frame during which Suzanne disappeared, a period during which Gilroy was in the vicinity but unaccounted for. Sniffer dogs had found indications of a dead body in the vicinity of Gilroy's car and also inside it. There was Gilroy's strange behavior after the murder, the air fresheners, the unscheduled trip to Argyll, the unusual route, the time and fuel unaccounted for. The police had also examined Gilroy's car and found damage to the suspension and vegetation stuck to its undercarriage, both indicators that he had driven off-road.

And there was one other detail, more abstruse, but nonetheless damning to David Gilroy. During the two weeks leading up to Suzanne's disappearance, he had harassed her with over 400 texts and voice messages. Yet, after 9 o'clock on the morning of May 4, 2010, there was not a single call. While everyone else in Suzanne's universe was fretting over her whereabouts and wellbeing, there was nothing from the man who claimed to love her, not even a text to ask, "Where are you?" or "I hope you're okay."

David Gilroy was convicted of Suzanne Pilley's murder in April 2012. He was sentenced to life in prison with a minimum term of 18 years. He continues to insist that he did not kill Suzanne and thus has never revealed the location of her body. Several additional searches have been conducted since 2012, the most recent in March 2018. All have come up empty.

Dressed to Kill

Karen Sharpe was getting her life back together. The attractive, 44-year-old mother of three had recently gone through a traumatic separation from her husband Richard, and was expecting an equally traumatic divorce. But tonight, July 14, 2000, Karen was putting all of that behind her. Tonight she'd accepted an invitation from her brother Jamie and his girlfriend to have dinner with friends and then enjoy a moonlight boat cruise around Gloucester Harbor, in affluent Essex County, Massachusetts.

Entrusting her two youngest children to the care of their regular babysitter, Karen left her home in Wenham at around 8:00 p.m. She returned at 11:40 after an enjoyable evening. Then, while Jamie went to check on 7-year-old Michael and 4-year-old Alexandra, while Karen stood in the foyer talking to the babysitter, a man entered the house through the unlocked front door. He was carrying a rifle. Jamie, in the adjacent TV room, heard his sister shout: "Oh God, no!" Then there was a single gunshot and the babysitter started screaming.

Jamie rushed back into the foyer, just in time to see the dark-clad man
disappear through the front door. Moments later, a car started up and
then raced away from the scene, tires squealing. But Jamie wasn't
interested in chasing down the attacker. His sole focus was Karen, who
was lying on the floor with blood spreading out around her. Already
she had lapsed into unconsciousness.

A frantic 911 call from Jamie Hatfield brought police and paramedics
racing towards the house. Karen was rushed to nearby Beverly
Hospital where trauma surgeons fought a desperate but ultimately
futile battle to save her. Karen had suffered a single bullet wound to
the back from a high-powered rifle. She died on the operating table. In
the meantime, Wenham police had issued an APB on the shooter,
identified by Jamie Hatfield. He was Dr. Richard Sharpe, Karen's
estranged husband.

Within hours of the shooting, Richard Sharpe's picture was staring out
from every media outlet in Massachusetts. Police in Wenham had
launched their first murder inquiry in 20 years, and a massive manhunt
was underway for the runaway dermatologist. But Dr. Sharpe wasn't at
his residence in nearby Gloucester, he wasn't at his medical offices or
at any of his usual haunts. Richard Sharpe, it appeared, had gone on
the run.

With the Massachusetts State police now called into the investigation,
the search parameters were extended to include the whole of
Massachusetts plus its surrounding states. The search would come to
an end 30 hours later when the fugitive was tracked to the Pine View
Lodge in Tuftonborough, New Hampshire, where he had taken a room

under his own name. He was captured without incident after officers forced him out into the open with teargas.

Extradited back to Massachusetts, Sharpe was arraigned for murder. And because he was clearly a flight risk, bail was denied. He was held initially at the Essex House of Correction but was soon transferred to Bridgewater State Hospital. Jailors feared that his bizarre behavior, spending hours at a time curled up in a fetal position on the concrete floor of his cell, made him a suicide risk. As investigators began looking into Sharpe's background, they would soon discover that bizarre behavior went with the territory.

Richard Sharpe was born on August 23, 1954 in Connecticut, the third of four children. His father, Benjamin, was a brutal man who inflicted both physical and emotional trauma on his offspring. The one exception was Richard's younger sister, Laurie, the only girl in the family. And that must have registered something in Richard's immature brain because, from the age of ten, he started to dress himself in his sister's clothes. It didn't stop the beatings, but nonetheless Richard had developed a liking for the way he looked, dressed as a girl. Soon he was saving up his pocket money, spending every penny of it on girls' clothing items. It was a fixation that would remain with him throughout his life.

Given his teenaged penchant for cross-dressing, it is perhaps unsurprising that Richard grew up with conflicting messages regarding his sexuality. But all of that was to change during his senior year at high school, when he met and fell in love with a pretty 17-year-old named Karen Hatfield. Over the objections of Karen's family, who found him rude and obnoxious, the two started dating, and Karen soon

fell pregnant. In 1973, she gave birth to a daughter, who they named
Shannon. A few months later, Richard and Karen were wed.

Despite the unplanned marriage and the responsibilities of parenthood,
both Richard and Karen were determined to continue their educations.
She attended nursing college while holding down two jobs and raising
her daughter. He obtained an engineering degree before deciding that
he wanted to be a doctor. In 1985, Richard was accepted into Harvard
Medical School, eventually graduating with honors, specializing in
dermatology. Thereafter, he was given a teaching post at the
prestigious university. At the same time, he invested in a laser hair
removal business, an undertaking that would eventually make him a
millionaire.

To the casual observer, Richard Sharpe's life must have looked like it
was on an unbroken upward trajectory. But the doctor's success
masked a dark persona, lurking just below the surface. Sharpe had
never shaken off his sexual identity issues and was still obsessed with
wearing women's clothing. Often he'd dress up in Karen's outfits, and
he even delved into his teenage daughter's wardrobe. If his obsession
had stopped there, it might have been classified as a harmless
diversion. But Sharpe went further. He regularly had all of his body
hair removed by laser at one of his clinics; he prescribed hormone pills
for himself; he started taking his wife's birth control pills so that he
could grow breasts; he had plastic surgery to make his nose more
feminine.

Even worse, Sharpe appeared to have inherited his father's penchant
for domestic violence. Karen suffered regular beatings and constant
verbal abuse. So too did their daughter. On one occasion, he locked

Karen in a room for 48 hours, beating her constantly over that period, inflicting such severe injuries that she ended up in the hospital.

Given this abuse, it is perhaps understandable that Karen began casting her eye elsewhere for affection. In April 1991, Richard returned early from work and found his wife in bed with another man. Flying into a rage, he picked up a fork and buried it in Karen's forehead, seriously injuring her. Karen was rushed to the hospital yet again while Richard was arrested and later admitted to a psychiatric facility. There he was diagnosed with various mental health issues, including depression and schizoid personality disorder.

The brutal attack perpetrated on Karen Sharpe would have ended most marriages. But Karen appears to have been a particularly resilient woman. Above all, she was determined to keep her family together. And so she gave in to Richard's contrite apologies, agreed to give it another shot, and withdrew the assault charges that had been laid.

For a time, things appeared to be getting back on an even keel. The Sharpe's moved to the exclusive enclave of Gloucester, Massachusetts and over the next few years had two more children, Michael, born 1992, and Alexandra, born in 1995. By 1997, Richard Sharpe had made his first million. Three years later, in 2000, he was worth more than $5 million.

But by then old habits had already re-established themselves in the marriage. Karen was again being subjected to physical and emotional abuse, and in February 2000, she decided that she had finally had enough. On February 28, she snuck out of the house in the middle of

the night, taking her children with her. The following day, she phoned
Richard and told him that she wanted a divorce. Before she'd even had
a chance to file a petition, he hired an attorney and started proceedings
of his own.

This, however, was a divorce with a twist. Throughout their marriage,
Richard had maintained total control over the couple's financial
affairs. That was until late 1999, when Richard became embroiled in a
bitter legal dispute and was sued by some of his competitors. Believing
that this might result in the courts attaching his assets, he'd moved
quickly, transferring $3 million in cash and property, including the
new family mansion in Wenham, into Karen's name. What this meant
was that, at the time of the divorce, Karen was worth more than
Richard.

To make matters worse for Richard, he discovered that Karen had
already moved on to a new relationship. And then he suffered a fall
down a flight of stairs at work, resulting in back injuries for which he
was prescribed a powerful painkiller.

And so to the night of the murder. Richard had been out that evening,
taking his new girlfriend, Paula Hiltz, a receptionist at his medical
practice, to a restaurant and then hitting several bars. He had
consumed a lot of alcohol and had also spent the evening popping his
prescription painkillers as though they were M&Ms. At around 10
p.m., while driving home, he had insisted that they stop off at Paula's
ex-boyfriend's house. The man had a large gun collection, and Sharpe
had tried to buy a 30-caliber rifle from him just a few weeks earlier.
On this occasion, Sharpe did not ask about buying the weapon.

Instead, he snuck it out with him when he left. Although it has never been found, this is likely the gun that killed Karen Sharpe.

Richard Sharpe appeared at Essex County Superior Court in November 2001, charged with the murder of his wife. Since Sharpe had never denied pulling the trigger, his defense team entered a plea of not guilty by reason of insanity. They then produced an expert witness who testified that Sharpe was suffering from numerous mental disorders, most of which could be traced back to the abuse he'd suffered as a child. Sharpe then took the stand in his own defense. He claimed that he could not remember shooting his wife and said that he'd felt as though he'd been losing his grip on reality in the days leading up to the murder.

Unfortunately for Dr. Sharpe, his actions in the aftermath of the murder did not support his testimony. If, as the expert witness had testified, he lacked the ability to tell right from wrong, why had he fled the scene, why had he disposed of the murder weapon, why had he gone on the run? These were not the actions of a man who had acted in a dissociative state. These were the deliberate acts of a criminal who understood both the gravity and consequences of his actions.

The jury agreed. On November 29, 2001, Richard Sharpe was convicted of first-degree murder and sentenced to life in prison without parole. He would serve just over eight years of that term before hanging himself in his cell on January 5, 2009.

Thus Always with Tyrants

On the morning of December 18, 1884, a neighbor of William Druse called on his ramshackle farmhouse near the village of Little Falls, in Herkimer County, New York. Druse, a local farmer, lived there with his wife, Roxalana (known as Roxy), his 19-year-old daughter, Mary, and his ten-year-old son, George. Frank Gates, William's 14-year-old nephew, also lived on the property and helped out with the farm work. This was a good thing since William Druse was known to be bone idle. He also had a reputation for being mean-spirited and for abusing his wife and children. Many wondered why Roxy, who at 42 years of age was 18 years younger than her husband, stayed with him.

Whatever business it was that had brought Druse's neighbor to his farm that morning has never been recorded. Neither was it concluded. As the man approached, he noticed that all of the windows had been covered with newspaper. He noticed also that a dense black smoke was issuing from the chimney, and as he got closer, he picked up the stench of it, the unmistakable reek of seared flesh. Although this spooked the visitor, he nonetheless rapped at the door. When there was no response from within, he decided to leave. He had by now gained the distinct impression that something bad was going on inside the house. His initial thought was that William had murdered his family and was at that very moment destroying their bodies in the fireplace.

That, however, would turn out to be inaccurate. Within days, Roxy Druse and her children were spotted in Little Falls, hale and hearty. There was no sign of William, though. When a curious shopkeeper asked about his whereabouts, Mrs. Druse said that he was in New York City conducting some or other business. This explanation was accepted without question.

But as the weeks went by and there was still no sign of William, the rumor mill began to crank. The story was that Roxy had murdered her husband and disposed of his body. This gained even more traction when the locals heard about the papered up windows and the foul-smelling smoke that had been seen coming from the chimney. When these stories reached the ears of Herkimer County district attorney A. B. Steele, he decided to launch an inquiry.

William's nephew, Frank Gates, was considered the most likely to break ranks on any secrets the family might be keeping. The 14-year-old was placed under arrest and then subjected to a brutal interrogation by the D.A., who demanded to know what had happened to William Druse. It did not take long before Frank cracked and admitted that William had been murdered. His Aunt Roxy had done the killing, he said, although he admitted that he, Mary, and 10-year-old George had all played a part.

According to Frank, it had all started on the morning of December 18 when William and Roxy were engaged in one of their frequent quarrels, this time over a grocery bill. Eventually, the argument became so vicious that Roxy had ordered Frank and George out of the room. Moments later, Frank heard a gunshot, then two more before he heard Roxy calling his name. He re-entered the room to find William on the floor, shot through the neck and clawing at his wounds in a vain attempt to stop the flow of blood. Roxy then handed him the gun and ordered him to shoot his uncle. Frank, terrified by "the look in her eyes," had complied, emptying the revolver.

But still William wouldn't die and, out of bullets now, Roxy reached for another weapon – an axe. "Oh, Roxy, don't!" William pleaded as she swung the blade and buried it in his skull. She then levered the axe loose and swung again. This time, William Druse had nothing to say on the matter. Then, as the horrified boy looked on, his aunt lifted the axe and used it to sever William's head. That took three strokes and she then decided that the blade was too dull and sent Frank and George outdoors to find a sharper one. By the time they returned, Roxy had already laid out a razor and a jackknife on the table. She then ordered him and George into another room, telling them to play a few games of checkers. In the meantime, she and her daughter, Mary, got to work dissecting William's body.

Most of the body parts, according to Frank, ended up being incinerated in the kitchen stove. The following day, Roxy ordered him to accompany her to Ball's swamp, about a half-mile from the house, where they disposed of the ashes and bone fragments. The axe that had ended William's life was discarded at the same location.

It was about as thorough a confession as the D.A. had ever taken. The following day, he took a posse of men out to the Druse farm and placed Roxalana Druse, her daughter Mary, and even 10-year-old George under arrest. At the same time, a team was sent into the swamp with Frank Gates as a guide. The possibility of finding any evidence seemed remote, but the weather worked in favor of the searchers. In the frigid temperatures, the ash and bone fragments had clumped together. The party was able to recover 20 small pieces of bone, the upper left tibia and both of William Druse's knee caps. They also found the murder weapon.

On January 17, Roxy Druse was brought before an inquest to determine whether there was sufficient evidence to put her on trial for murder. This, of course, was a mere formality. Once the jurors heard of the frequent quarrels between husband and wife, of the black smoke seen pouring from the chimney, of Roxy's lies regarding her husband's whereabouts, they were already decided. And that was before Frank Gates took the stand. Frank told essentially the same story that he'd told the D.A., and it was damning to Roxy.

One interesting detail did, however, emerge at the inquest. Called to testify, 10-year-old George Druse mentioned that his uncle, Charley Gates (Frank's father), had also been present at the time of the murder. Oddly, the D.A. chose not to act on this information. Charles Gates was never indicted. It would later emerge that it was he, rather than Roxy, who'd been the main player in the murder.

Roxalana Druse was given the opportunity to address the inquest, but she chose not to take the stand. What could she have said that would have swayed the jury? That she had endured years of beatings and humiliation and had finally decided to fight back? That a woman had every right to defend herself? In that era, it would not have made a jot of difference. Roxy was charged with causing her husband's death by shooting him and striking him with an axe. Mary Druse, George Druse, and Frank Gates were charged with aiding and abetting her.

The trial of Roxalana Druse got underway on September 24, 1885, and lasted two weeks. The testimony primarily covered the same grounds as had been addressed at the inquest but with additional exhibits, including two blood-stained floorboards that had been pried loose from the Druse farmstead. Since the state had such a strong case, the only avenue open to Roxy's lawyer was to argue self-defense, after years of physical and mental abuse. As we have already noted, this was considered a questionable argument in those less enlightened times. It may, however, have gained some traction had Roxy taken the stand to describe her plight to the jury. Unfortunately, she did not. Whether that was on advice from counsel or due to her own obstinacy is not recorded. Either way, it was fatal to her case. Roxy Druse was found guilty of murder and sentenced to hang.

Justice moved swiftly in those days, with convicted murderers often put to death within weeks of sentencing. In Roxy's case, however, there was an appeals process lasting 18 months. During that time, the case provoked fierce debate, both for and against the condemned woman. One man offered to go to the gallows in her place; another offered $10 for the privilege of springing the lever that would send Roxy to her death.

One group that was particularly vocal in its support of Roxalana Druse was the fledgling women's rights movement. It argued, quite accurately, that Roxy's case had not been heard before a jury of her peers, since the panel had been comprised solely of men. It also argued that since women did not have the right to vote, Roxy's status in society was similar to that of a minor and therefore she could not legally be put to death by the state. Again, it is difficult to argue with this logic. In the end, however, it made no difference.

Roxalana Druse was put to death at the Herkimer county jail on February 28, 1887, in front of 25 witnesses. New York at that time had dispensed with the traditional gallows that involved the condemned person falling through a trapdoor. Its method (supposedly more efficient) was to yank the condemned person into the air using a counterweight. Like the more commonly used gallows, this was supposed to snap the condemned's neck, killing them instantly. In Roxalana Druse's case, it went horribly wrong. She was left dangling at the end of the rope for 15 minutes, slowly asphyxiating. Several of those present were said to have been deeply traumatized by the spectacle.

But should Roxalana Druse have been executed at all? After her death, her spiritual advisor, Dr. Powell, revealed details of what Roxy had told him while she was awaiting execution. She said that it was her brother-in-law, Charles Gates, who had hatched the murder plot. Roxy admitted firing the first shot at William but said that it was Charles (and not his son, Frank) who had finished the job. She also contended that William was already dead (or dying) when she struck him with the axe. That act had been a response to the years of abuse she'd suffered at his hands. Roxy hadn't implicated Charles because she was grateful to him for releasing her from her untenable situation. Hanging, she said, was preferable to spending the rest of her life with William Druse.

Roxalana Druse was the last woman to be hanged by the state of New York. Her botched execution was a major reason behind the move to the "more humane" electric chair.

After the Fall

At sixteen minutes past midnight on the morning of March 1, 2001, a 999 call came in to the emergency services in Balbriggan, a small town some 20 miles to the north of Dublin, Ireland. The caller was a man who was sobbing pitifully, saying that his wife had fallen down the stairs and wasn't moving and didn't appear to be breathing. Calming the man down, the operator asked for his name and was told that it was Colin Whelan. Then she obtained the address and dispatched an ambulance. Keeping Whelan on the line, she instructed him in how to perform CPR and heart massage on his wife. Whelan said that he'd try, but minutes later said that he'd done as instructed and was getting no response. By then it was 12:30 a.m. and the ambulance had arrived.

Paramedics who entered the home spotted Mary Whelan immediately, lying in a crumpled heap at the bottom of the steep staircase, a quilt covering her body. Standing close by, still holding the phone, was her husband Colin. As the EMTs got to work trying to revive Mary, Colin repeated his story, saying that he'd heard several thumps and then found his wife lying at the foot of the stairs.

The story, however, sounded suspicious to the medics. They did not
think that the position of the body was consistent with someone who
had suffered a fall. They also couldn't understand why Mary had been
covered with a quilt. The 999 dispatcher would certainly not have told
Whelan to do so. And Whelan's assertion that he had tried CPR on his
wife was a lie. Mary had blood on her face which would have
transferred to Colin had he applied his mouth to hers. Yet his face was
clean. Even more telling was Whelan's attitude, which was hardly
consistent with a distraught husband. As Mary was being wheeled
towards the waiting ambulance, all he could think to say was, "Is she
dead?"

Mary Whelan was rushed to Beaumont Hospital in Dublin but was
pronounced dead at 1:25 a.m., just over an hour after her husband had
made the frantic 999 call. When night nurse Catherine Galvin went to
ask Colin to clarify details of Mary's fall, he recited his story in a
disinterested drone, his cool demeanor at odds with the tragedy that
had just befallen him. Then Galvin noticed something. Whelan's top
shirt buttons were undone and the nurse could see scratches on his
chest. That was when it was decided to call the Garda (the Irish
police).

Superintendent Tom Gallagher arrived at the hospital soon after.
Whelan appeared surprised to be suddenly faced with a police
detective, but he was nonetheless cooperative and willingly removed
his shirt when asked to do so. He seemed oblivious to the fact that he'd
been scratched. When the scratches were pointed out to him, he
suddenly remembered something that he'd failed to mention during the
many retellings of his story. He now said that Mary had still been
conscious when he'd reached her and had lashed out at him as he'd

tried to help her. Gallagher didn't believe him. He also knew that a fall down a carpeted staircase was seldom fatal unless the victim broke his or her neck, which was not the case with Mary Whelan. At this point no one knew for certain how Mary had died, although the bluish tinge to her lips suggested asphyxiation. All doubt would be removed by the subsequent autopsy. Mary Whelan had been strangled.

Colin, however, was not about to admit to anything. Asked to come down to police headquarters, he repeated his earlier story about what had happened. According to him, he'd been downstairs watching television while Mary was taking a shower upstairs. He'd heard a number of dull thuds and had rushed into the hallway where he'd found his wife lying at the bottom of the stair case.

No one believed Whelan's story, but it was up to the police to prove him a liar. And the clues were not long in coming. A forensic examination of the house found blood spatters on the skirting board and carpet in the master bedroom. There were also traces of blood in the bathroom sink. Then there was the belt from Colin Whelan's dressing gown, which appeared to have been stretched and also had a bloodstain on it. Detectives believed that this was the murder weapon. They reckoned that a towel had been placed between the victim's flesh and the ligature in an effort to conceal evidence of strangulation. Unfortunately for the killer, the towel had slipped in the course of the struggle, leaving behind the small ligature mark that had been found on Mary's neck during the autopsy.

The police now had a good idea of what had happened in the Whelan household on the night of the murder. They believed that Colin Whelan had attacked his wife after she got out of the shower and changed into her pajamas. He'd struck from behind, wrapping his custom ligature of towel and dressing gown belt around her neck and pulling it tight. Mary, however, had managed to turn and face her attacker, lashing out with her nails and raking him across the chest. But despite her valiant effort, she never stood a chance. Mary was just 5-foot-4, her husband over six foot. Slowly, he'd choked the life out of her, impassively increasing the force until her face turned blue and blood began seeping from her nose. Then, after she'd blacked out, he'd dragged her down the stairs (carpet burns on her back verified this) and left her in a heap at the bottom. Then he'd executed the next part of his devious plan, covering her body with a quilt and turning up the heat in the house to maintain her body temperature. He needed to do this because he waited a half hour before calling the emergency services. He wanted to be sure that there would be no chance of paramedics saving Mary's life.

Those were the mechanics of this dreadful crime. What the Garda still did not understand was why. Why would a man murder his wife of just six months in such brutal fashion? As is so often the case, it came down to two things – sex and money.

Colin Whelan had met Mary Gough while she was working as a barmaid at the Huntsman Inn, a pub he regularly drank at. Mary, 19 years old at the time, was attracted to the tall, handsome Colin, but he appeared shy, and it was several months before he eventually asked her out and the couple started dating. Colin was an intelligent and entrepreneurial young man who had started his own IT company shortly after graduating from Gormanston College. At the time he met Mary, he had just one client. He was employed as a full-time computer analyst by Irish Permanent, one of Ireland's largest banks.

Colin's relationship with Mary became serious very quickly, and it was almost expected that they would eventually marry. But then, in 1995, Colin suddenly informed Mary that it was over between them. He gave no reason for his decision, leaving the young woman so distraught that she became physically ill. Mary, though, was a fighter, and she eventually recovered, landing a prestigious job as a secretary with an Irish film company. There, her hard work and organizational skills were so appreciated that she was offered a promotion and a transfer to the company offices in Scotland. The only reason that she turned it down was because she still harbored hope of a reconciliation with Colin.

And that dream was realized when a contrite Colin contacted her, admitted that he'd made a mistake, and begged her to take him back. Mary, of course, did so without hesitation, even moving into the house that Colin had recently bought in Balbriggan. The house featured a particularly steep staircase, and Colin would often joke that one of them would take a tumble sooner or later.

That much-anticipated accident never materialized, but another did. On January 31, 1997, Colin Whelan was driving his car along a road in nearby Gormanstown when he was involved in a head-on collision. Whelan was unhurt in the crash as was the other driver. However, the passenger in the other vehicle, 61-year-old Elizabeth Murphy, was killed, resulting in Whelan being charged with dangerous driving. He'd ultimately be acquitted on that charge, although the accident left him emotionally scarred. It was only the support of his loving girlfriend that pulled him through.

Eventually, in 2000, Colin asked Mary to marry him, and Mary said yes. That was when the trouble started. At the wedding reception, Mary's mother found her daughter alone and crying, refusing to say why when her mother asked. Almost immediately after the nuptials, Mary's close-knit family started to see less and less of her. When they did see Mary, they noticed that she appeared unhappy, that she wore no make-up and had on particularly frumpy clothes. They suspected that Colin might be behind this transformation, and they were right. He'd taken control of his wife's life, withholding affection, keeping her away from those she loved, ordering her to dress in a way that would make her unattractive to anyone else. No one could have predicted, though, that he would cause her physical harm.

But Whelan had harmed his wife, and the police believed that they had the evidence to prove it. What they didn't know yet was the level of premeditation that had gone into this sickening crime. That would only come to light once the Garda obtained a search warrant for Colin Whelan's computer.

Whelan was, of course, a computer programmer. But he appears to have had little understanding of other aspects of computing. He did not know, for example, that deleting the search history does not eradicate all traces of the sites he'd visited, that a record of the browsing history remains on the hard drive.

And Whelan's browsing history was interesting. He had conducted searches using terms like "asphyxiation" and "how to get away with murder" and "how to maintain body temperature." He'd also researched several murderers and appeared particularly interested in Henry Louis Wallace, the American serial killer known as the

"Charlotte Strangler." Wallace was adept at making his victims' deaths look like accidents and used two ploys which showed up later in Mary Whelan's murder. He commonly used a towel to disguise ligature marks, and he covered his victims with blankets to confuse investigators as to the time of death.

What is even more chilling about the searches carried out by Whelan is the time frame in which he conducted his research. He'd started even before his wedding to Mary, meaning that on the day they took their vows, he was already planning to kill her. To what purpose? For the £400,000 insurance policy he'd taken out on her life. Whelan was also fond of trawling adult hook-up sites and had already struck up an online relationship with a divorced mother of two. They had recently been discussing meeting in person.

Colin Whelan was arrested on April 10, 2001, and charged with murdering his wife. Granted bail, he swore that he would clear his name. But Whelan was no fool. He knew that the evidence against him made an acquittal extremely unlikely.

And so Whelan ran. First he applied for a passport under the name of his neighbor, Martin Sweeney. Then he drove his car to Howth Head, a range of steep cliffs to the north of Dublin and the site of several suicides over the years. Abandoning his car at this spot (with the obvious intention of suggesting that he'd taken his own life), he boarded a train to Belfast, Northern Ireland. From there, he flew to Spain and made his way to the beautiful Mediterranean island of Mallorca.

Whelan settled in Magaluf and got a job as bartender at the Squadron Bar in Puerto Portals. This exclusive tavern was frequented by millionaires and jet-setters, and Whelan felt safe here, certain that he'd go undetected. Over time, he began to let his guard down and started a relationship with an Englishwoman named Katie Wilcox. He also began partying at the pubs and nightspots in the more touristy town of Santa Ponsa. It was here that he was spotted by an Irish tourist who later reported the sighting to the Garda. After being at large for a year and four months, Whelan was arrested and returned to Ireland to face the music.

Whelan's capture was big news in his homeland, and his April 2005 trial was much anticipated in the media. However, at his first court appearance, Whelan took everyone by surprise by entering a guilty plea. He was subsequently sentenced to life in prison, the harshest term available under Irish law for one of the most cold-blooded murders committed on those shores.

The Honeymoon Murder

It reads like something out of an Agatha Christie novel, except that in this case you have to substitute Ms. Christie's perceptive amateur sleuth, Jane Marple, for a middle-aged spinster by the name of Evelyn Crossley. Miss Crossley was a frequent visitor to the Borrowdale Gates Hotel, a luxury resort situated on the southern shores of Derwent Water in England's Lake District. Set within the tranquil, stunning scenery of the Borrowdale Valley, the hotel was a regular getaway for the famous and well-heeled. It was also a popular destination for honeymooners.

Take the couple sitting across from Miss Crossley at breakfast – young, handsome and quite obviously in love. She'd first noticed them at dinner the previous evening and, like everyone else in the room, had found her eyes drawn to them. They looked like a pair of Hollywood movie stars, he in stylish dinner jacket, she in glamorous gown and dazzling jewelry. Being of a more curious persuasion than the other guests, Miss Crossley had simply had to know more. And so, when she'd found the couple enjoying a nightcap in the lounge later that

evening, she'd walked over and introduced herself. That was when she
learned that the glamour was no mere façade.

He was Chung Yi-miao, a 28-year-old American lawyer of Chinese
birth; she was Siu Wai-sheung, a Boston University educated heiress
from the island of Macao. The couple had met at a dance in New York
in 1927, while Wai was visiting the United States to attend an auction
of Chinese jade and objets d'art. Thereafter had followed a whirlwind
romance before they'd married in New York in May 1928. They'd
then embarked on an extensive honeymoon tour of the States before
boarding a luxury liner bound for Britain. After exploring Scotland for
a week, they'd come to the Lake District, a fittingly tranquil way to
wind down their first trip together as a couple.

All of this was deeply fascinating to Miss Crossley, a way to
experience, by proxy, the romance that had never quite materialized in
her own life. Yet there was something about Chung that she found
decidedly unnerving – the way his smile never quite seemed to reach
his eyes; the sideways glances he cast towards his wife while she was
talking. To Miss Crossley, the expression he wore looked decidedly
like contempt, perhaps even loathing.

But that was misconception surely. The couple were, after all, on their
honeymoon. After bidding them goodnight and retiring to her room,
Miss Crossley ran over the evening's events in her mind and decided
that she was being silly. Now, sitting across from the couple at
breakfast, she saw that she had indeed been mistaken. Chung could not
have been more attentive to his bride.

Tuesday, June 19, 1928, was a glorious sunny day in the Lakes. After breakfast, as Miss Crossley sat down on the terrace to read the morning newspapers, she spotted the Chungs going for a stroll, walking hand in hand. After returning for lunch, they set off again, with Chung wearing an elegant, fawn topcoat to ward off the chill breeze that had sprung up off the water. He was still wearing that coat when he returned to the hotel at 4 o'clock. Wai, however, was nowhere to be seen. Miss Crossley overheard Chung telling a maid that she'd gone alone into the nearby town of Keswick to buy some warm clothes.

By dinner, Wai had still not put in an appearance. Concerned, Miss Crossley approached Chung, who was dining alone, and asked him about his wife. Somewhat abruptly, Chung informed her that his wife was a seasoned traveler and would soon find her way home. When Miss Crossley pointed out that there was only one evening bus from Keswick, he told her that that would not be a problem since Wai would take a cab.

But by ten that evening, no cab from Keswick had borne Mrs. Chung back to the hotel and now, at last, her husband began to show some concern. He went down to the reception desk and asked if it would be advisable for him to phone the police at this time. Yet when the receptionist asked whether Chung would like her to dial the number for him, he declined, saying he'd call from his room. Except that he never made that call. He went straight to bed and fell asleep, oblivious to the drama that was unfolding at that time, just a mile from the hotel.

Earlier that evening, a farmer named Thomas Wilson had been making his way through a wood named Cumma Catta, when he spotted a

woman lying on the ground beside a pond. On reaching his
destination, the local pub, Wilson struck up a conversation with an off-
duty policeman, Constable Pendelbury, telling him what he'd seen. He
hadn't wanted to disturb the woman, he said, because she was
"sleeping so peaceful."

But to Pendelbury, this didn't sound right. Dusk was falling and it was
chilly outside, hardly the kind of weather in which someone would
decide to take a snooze outdoors. Abandoning his pint at the bar, the
police officer took a couple of men and went to check on the woman.
They found Wai lying in the exact spot Wilson had described. One
look told Pendelbury that she was dead. There was a thin white cord
pulled tightly around her throat and blood on her mouth. Her clothes
had also been disarranged, with her skirt pulled up and her underwear
torn. An expensive, diamond-encrusted watch still decorated her wrist,
but bruises on her fingers suggested that rings had been violently
removed. All of this pointed to a murderer motivated by rape and
robbery.

Chung Yi-miao, who had retired to bed without bothering to inform
the police of his wife's disappearance, was roused from sleep in the
early morning hours. On hearing that his wife had been found dead, his
response was a less than convincing show of angst: "How terrible! My
wife assaulted, robbed and murdered!" This was particularly
interesting to the police since no one had mentioned at this point that
Siu Wai-sheung had been assaulted or robbed. The police had not even
told Chung that they suspected murder.

The evidence soon began to stack up against Chung. First there was
the blood found on his fawn coat (he claimed this was "from New

York" without offering an additional explanation); then there were his wife's missing rings, found hidden in a camera film canister in his possession. Chung's explanation for this was that his wife often hid things in "peculiar places."

The police were by now certain that Chung Yi-miao was their man. However, they were dealing with a wily customer. As a lawyer, Chung knew exactly how the game was played. The police could suspect all they wanted, but without motive and evidence, he would breeze right out of there and they'd be unable to lay a hand on him. This was where Borrowdale's own Miss Marple came to the rescue.

Evelyn Crossley had a keen eye for detail and a solid understanding of human nature. She was able to fill the police in on Chung's odd demeanor towards his wife and his apparent lack of concern after her disappearance. She was also able to provide details of the couple's movements since she'd seen them heading in the direction of Cumma Catta together and seen Chung emerge from those woods alone. Aside from that, there was one unique insight that she offered into the apparent motive for the murder. She said that she found it odd that Wai had been both sexually assaulted and robbed. "The last person you'd suspect of having those motives would be the husband," she said. "That, to me, makes it the perfect cover."

That line of reasoning would form a major theme of the prosecution's case during Chung Yi-miao's trial. It was argued that Chung's real motive was financial, that he had married Wai with the intention of killing her and inheriting her fortune. Support for this theory was presented in a note, written in Chinese, that had been found in his possession. "Be sure to do it on the ship," he'd written, then "Don't do it on the ship," then "Again consider on arrival in Europe."

Chung could offer no explanation for the meaning of these notes. Instead, his defense team blamed the murder on a couple of mysterious "Orientals" who, according to Chung, had tracked them all the way from America. The defense even produced a witness who testified that he'd seen "two suspicious looking Chinese men" hanging around Keswick on the day of the murder.

This testimony made little impression on the jury who found Chung Yi-miao guilty. Judge Humphreys then donned the black cap and sentenced Chung to hang for the "truly diabolical and calculated murder." Chung was put to death at Manchester's Strangeways Prison on December 6, 1928, protesting his innocence to the end.

Michigan Deliverance

In 1972, director John Boorman introduced us to a movie classic. *Deliverance*, based on the acclaimed novel by James Dickey, tells the story of a quartet of city boys who set off on a canoeing trip through the Georgia wilderness and find themselves hunted by a group of psychopathic locals. With Burt Reynolds and John Voight in the starring roles, the movie is a dark and nightmarish fable, shocking in the raw savagery it depicts. It also finds a counterpart in real life. This story happened, not in Georgia, but in the woods of northern Michigan in 1985.

David Tyll and Brian Ognjan were best friends. The pair had first met in junior high and had struck up a close bond, one that had endured into adulthood. By 1985, when our story takes place, both men were 27 years old. David had married and was living in St. Clair Shores, Michigan, where he worked in his father-in-law's business as a machinist. Brian lived some 20 miles away in Troy, with his steady girlfriend. He earned his living as an auto mechanic.

David's family, at that time, owned a hunting cabin on Base Line Road near White Cloud, Michigan and it had become somewhat of a tradition for him and Brian to head down there each November for a weekend of deer hunting. In truth, neither man was a particularly keen hunter. The weekend was more of an excuse to blow off steam, to get falling down drunk and trade stories of the old days, to enjoy the primal experience of hanging out in the woods without the constraints of wives, girlfriends or family.

Thus it was on the weekend of 22-24 November, 1985. On Friday afternoon, November 22, Brian arrived at David's house, and the men loaded their gear into David's black Ford Bronco. David kissed his wife goodbye and told her that he'd see her on Sunday night. Then the friends hit the road.

But David didn't return that Sunday. He also didn't call, which was quite unlike him. After a round of phone calls to friends and family, his wife spent a fretful night waiting to hear from him before reporting him missing on Monday morning. The local police then made some calls and learned that David and Brian had been seen at several locations during the weekend, although none of them were near White Cloud. It seemed that they had never made it to the cabin. They certainly had not applied down there for a hunting license.

Sightings of David and Brian appeared to be centered on the Mio/Lake Houghton area. One local confirmed that two men matching their descriptions had stopped and asked him for directions. Most reports, however, were from taverns along the route. These suggested that David and Brian had been drinking heavily. The last confirmed sighting was at a bar called Linker's Lost Creek Lodge in Mio. According to patrons of that establishment, the two men had been drunk when they'd entered the bar and had consumed several more drinks while they were there. By the time they'd left, they had been barely able to stand.

This, of course, put a different spin on things. The woods of northern Michigan are dense and dangerous, especially during hunting season when they bristle with marksmen of varying skill levels. Two men, unfamiliar with the area, drunk, and driving a vehicle along the labyrinth of backroads, were just looking for trouble. They might easily have veered off the road and ended up in one of the many deep ponds in the region; they might have gotten lost, fallen into a ravine or been hit by stray bullets.

A search was therefore arranged without delay, one that would ultimately cover hundreds of square miles and employ aircraft, cadaver dogs, and divers. Dozens of lakes and rivers were trawled, fields were dug up, aerial searches conducted using ground-penetrating radar. In addition, state and county police interviewed hundreds of locals and pursued numerous leads. As the situation became more and more dire, they even followed up on tips from self-declared psychics. All of this came to nothing. As the days drifted into weeks, and the weeks into months, there seemed less and less chance of finding David or Brian alive. There was not even a trace of their vehicle. It was almost as though they had fallen off the edge of the earth.

And yet, the disappearance of David Tyll and Brian Ognjan should have been easily resolved. Their fate was an open secret in Mio, where everyone already knew that they were dead. It was also no secret who had killed them.

Raymond "J.R." Duvall and Donald "Coco" Duvall were as feared in Mio as they were reviled. They were two of the seven Duvall brothers, a close-knit clan who held the small Michigan town in a grip of terror. Quick to violence and with little concern as to who they targeted, the brothers lived in rundown trailers and ramshackle cabins in the woods. They raised pigs and poached fish and game. They were also petty criminals, illegally siphoning electricity from the grid and making their living off stolen cars which they chopped up and sold for parts. They were heavy drinkers and barroom brawlers, always spoiling for a fight. A stray word or glance could put you in the hospital, and so locals knew to keep their eyes diverted and their voices low when the Duvalls were around.

David Tyll and Brian Ognjan, of course, would not have known this. Drunk and perhaps talking too loud and flashing their cash, they would instantly have become a target for the Duvalls. Their innocent high-jinx in a Michigan barroom would end up getting them killed and trigger an unspoken conspiracy of silence in Mio, one that would remain unbroken for eighteen years. It was only the persistence of a Michigan State Police detective that eventually convinced an eyewitness to the murder to speak up. Only then would the dreadful truth be revealed.

Barbra Boudro was almost as well-known in Mio as the Duvall brothers. She was a familiar sight at Linker's, propping up the bar at all hours, usually with a large vodka tonic at her elbow. Barbra had been sitting in her usual spot on the night that David Tyll and Brian

Ognjan stumbled through the doors of her favorite watering hole. She'd already consumed a number of beverages that night, but like the other regular patrons, she cringed at the rowdy behavior of the two young men. The Duvalls were in the house and that could only mean trouble.

Still, the Duvalls appeared to be showing an unusual amount of restraint on this particular night. By the time Barbra left the bar about an hour later, they still had made no move towards the young men who were still laughing and whooping it up. J.R. and Coco did cast the odd poisonous glance in their direction, but that was about the extent of their interaction.

After leaving Linker's, Barbra walked to a friend's house, a short distance away. There her friend poured them a night cap, but they had not yet finished their drinks when they heard voices from the adjacent field. One of those voices sounded desperate, pleading. The other was easily recognizable. It was J.R. Duvall. "You boys picked the wrong place to party," he was saying.

Barbra crept to the window, parted the drapes slightly and peered out. There was a full moon that night, and the scene was also illuminated by the outside houselights. She could clearly see the two young men from the bar, kneeling in the dirt. Hovering over them were J.R. and Coco Duvall, Coco holding a baseball bat. One of the young men was begging them to let him and his friend go, but those pleas fell on deaf ears. As Barbra watched in horror, Coco swung the bat at one of the men, connecting with such force that, according to Barbra's later testimony, "his head just disappeared." As the man collapsed into the dirt, his friend staggered to his feet and tried to make a run for it. But he was quickly run to ground and dragged back. "Look, he peed his pants," Coco chuckled. Then he and his brother started punching, kicking and stomping the man, and Barbra could no longer bear to watch. She let the drapes fall back into place and crept off to bed. Despite her inebriated state, she hardly slept a wink that night.

Over the weeks that followed, J.R and Coco Duvall regularly held court at Linker's, boasting to anyone within earshot about how they had beaten their victims to death, cut up their bodies and fed them to their pigs because "even pigs gotta eat." They'd continue their boasts even when there were State troopers in town, asking questions about the missing men. The implication was clear. Anyone who spoke out against the Duvalls would end up as pig food. And so those who knew (which amounted to just about everyone in town) said nothing. It was only when Barbra Boudro found the courage to tell her story that the wall of silence broke. Then others came forward to tell what they knew, about how the Duvalls had followed the strangers out into the parking lot on that fateful November night; about how they'd later boasted about the murders; about how they'd chopped up their victims and turned them into pig feed.

Donald and Raymond Duvall were arrested and charged with murder. Despite the prosecution being unable to produce the bodies of the victims, the murder weapon, or any forensic evidence, they were convicted and sentenced to life in prison without the possibility of parole. "This was the stuff of horror stories," an officer involved in the investigation would later remark. "It was three levels below Deliverance."

Mr. Saturday Night

On the evening of July 15, 1973, Sandra Newton stormed out of a pub
in the village of Britton Ferry, South Wales, after an argument with her
boyfriend. The 16-year-old then stuck out a thumb to hitch a ride to
her home in Neath, just a few miles away. She was never seen alive
again. The following morning, a dog walker came across her corpse,
discarded in a drainage ditch in nearby woods. A strip of her skirt had
been torn off and was tightly twisted around her neck, indicating that
she'd been strangled. This was later confirmed by the pathologist, who
also determined that Sandra had engaged in sexual activity on the
night she died. The only other clue left at the scene was a tire track,
imprinted in the mud. Unfortunately, it was from a very common
brand and size.

But the police were not initially too concerned about that. After
retracing Sandra's steps and learning about the altercation at the pub,
they had a suspect in their sights – the boyfriend Sandra had argued
with. He was easy to track down and turned out to be a married man.
Questioned by police, he admitted to consensual sex with Sandra on
the night of the murder. However, he denied killing her. According to

him, he'd followed Sandra out of the pub but had soon returned to his pint after she refused to talk to him. The police weren't sure that they believed him, but other bar patrons backed up his story. And there was another problem with the theory of the boyfriend as killer. He didn't own a car and didn't even have a driver's license. Whoever had killed Sandra had driven her to her doom.

Months passed with hardly any progress in the Newton murder inquiry. Then, in September 1973, the South Wales police had an even more shocking crime to deal with. Geraldine Hughes and Pauline Floyd were friends and co-workers at a local sewing machine factory. On the evening of Saturday, September 16, the two sixteen-year-olds had taken a bus into Swansea, the largest town in the area. They had spent the night at the popular Top Rank nightclub, leaving at around 1 a.m. At this hour, the buses had stopped running, leaving the girls with two options: take a cab or hitchhike. Since a cab would have cost them £4 and they only earned £16 a week, they decided to hitch a ride.

By now, it had started to drizzle, and so the girls took shelter at a bus stop while they cast hopeful looks down the abandoned stretch of road. Motorist Philip O'Connor spotted them there at around 1:15 and was thinking about pulling over to pick them up when a white car appeared out of nowhere, cut across him and skidded to a halt next to the girls. The car, O'Connor would later tell police, was an Austin 1100. Although he didn't get a good look at the driver, O'Connor would describe the man as having dark, bushy hair and a moustache.

Pauline and Geraldine did not make it home that night. They were found at around 10 a.m. the next morning, in a wooded copse just off the Jersey Marine Road near the town of Llandarcy. Both girls had been strangled with a ligature, a five-foot length of rope that was found near the bodies. They had also been bludgeoned and had suffered serious head wounds. The medical examiner would later confirm that they'd both been raped.

Based on evidence found at the scene, the police were able to form a theory about how the crime had been committed. The girls had quite obviously been driven to the location where they'd been forced to undress. The killer had then raped both of them before ordering them to put their clothes on. He'd then attacked Pauline, beating her unconscious with some object. This had given Geraldine the chance to make a run for it, but she covered just 50 yards before being run to ground, beaten and then strangled to death. The killer then returned to finish Pauline off before leaving the scene. How had he managed to maintain control over both girls during the rapes? The police believed that he'd used the girls' friendship to his advantage. ("If you run, your friend dies.")

The brutal double homicide sent shock waves through South Wales and beyond. Soon the national newspapers had picked up the story and were reporting that a serial killer was on the loose, one who they dubbed the "Saturday Night Strangler." According to the tabloids, the man who'd killed Pauline and Geraldine was also the killer of Sandra Newton, who'd been strangled two months earlier. The police weren't so sure. Many on the force still believed that Sandra's boyfriend was responsible.

Nonetheless, a massive task team was assembled, involving over 150 detectives and uniformed officers. They had their work cut out for them. Llandarcy lies at the center of a major industrial belt with

several large steel plants and oil refineries, employing thousands of
men. Nearby is the port of Swansea, with international shipping
arriving and departing daily. Also at that time, the M4 freeway was
under construction, an operation that employed a huge work force.
Any of these workers might be the killer they were looking for, or he
might he a local man from anywhere in the Swansea valley, Neath or
Port Talbot.

There was, however, one solid clue the police were pursuing, the white
Austin 1100. Philip O'Connor had seen the girls getting into such a
vehicle, and motorists had spotted a similar car parked at the side of
the road, close to where the bodies were later found. No one had taken
note of the license plate number, but it was something to go on at least.

Unfortunately, it was another mammoth task. There were thousands of
similar vehicles registered in the area, and each owner had to be
interviewed and eliminated from the inquiry. One of those who was
questioned was a 32-year-old nightclub bouncer named Joseph
Kappen. Although he was a good physical match for the man seen by
Philip O'Connor, Kappen had an alibi. His wife said that he'd been
home all night. His white Austin was also non-operational. It had
engine trouble and was up on blocks. Although not entirely eliminated,
Kappen was relegated to the lower reaches of a potential suspect pool
which would swell to nearly 35,000.

By mid-1974, the murder inquiry was being dragged down under the
weight of the paperwork it had generated. Boxes of statements, index
cards, and pieces of evidence stood stacked at police headquarters,
evidence that the task force had no chance of evaluating in this pre-
computer age. With very little possibility of a successful resolution,

the task team was scaled down. Eventually, there were just two detectives, working on scraps of new information that came in. Everyone else was reassigned, while statements, notes, and physical evidence was boxed up and shipped to Sandfields police station in Port Talbot. It would there remain for nearly 30 years. Fortunately, someone had the foresight to send the key pieces of forensic evidence, including the victims' underwear, to the Home Office's forensic science labs in Chepstow, where it was kept under optimal conditions.

During the mid-1980s, the breakthrough investigative tool of DNA "fingerprinting" announced its arrival by ending the career of fledgling serial killer, Colin Pitchfork. Over the years that followed, DNA became an essential component of the investigators' armory. By 1998, the method had become refined enough to be applied to low quality samples. That triggered a spate of cold case investigations and the conviction of many criminals who had evaded the law for decades.

One of the first UK cases to which the new Low Copy Number DNA test was applied was that of the Saturday Night Strangler. Items of clothing belonging to Geraldine Hughes and Pauline Floyd were sent to a specialist lab in Birmingham where it would take two years before technicians were able to separate the killer's DNA from that of his victims. Once the profile was extracted, it was run against the UK's National DNA Database, which at that time held around 1.7 million profiles of convicted criminals. Unfortunately, the DNA of the Saturday Night Strangler was not among them.

At this point, the authorities might well have given up and moved on to cases that were more easily solved. To their credit, they did not, instead assembling a cold case team to review the original case files and compile a list of suspects from whom DNA might be obtained for comparison. As with everything about this investigation, that was easier said than done.

The cold case team involved just three men, Detective Chief Inspector Paul Bethell, who had worked as a rookie cop on the original investigation, and two veteran detectives approaching retirement age, Phil Rees and Geraint Bale. A fourth investigator, John Grey, was later added to the team, but the task facing them was nigh on impossible. Their budget was only enough to cover 500 DNA tests. That meant that they had to whittle down the list of 35,000 names to just 500 likely suspects.

Over the next eight months, Detectives Rees, Bale and Grey spent every minute of their working lives cooped up in a tiny room going through boxes of moldering old evidence. To help them narrow down their list, a behavioral scientist was asked to draw up a profile of the killer. That profile described him as white, late 20s to mid-30s, and a local man. He would have a history of petty crime stretching back to his youth. He'd also possibly have arrests for assault and for animal cruelty. He'd be an unskilled worker, involved in a troubled marriage or relationship. A loner, he would enjoy solitary pursuits and hobbies which did not require him to interact with other people.

Drawing on this profile, the cold case team was eventually able to complete the near-impossible task of whittling down the list to the 500 most likely suspects. Now an equally daunting job awaited them, tracking down the men on that list. Thirty years had passed since the murders. People had moved on, emigrated, changed their names, died.

Whole areas had been redeveloped. Streets that had once stood no longer existed.

Nonetheless, the detectives got to work. Within eight months, they'd tracked down 353 of the men on their list, one as far afield as New Zealand. All of the men had willingly submitted a sample and all had been ruled out.

One of those who hadn't been tested was Joseph Kappen. The reason for that was simple. When detectives knocked on the door at his last known address in August 2001, they were told by his former wife that he had died of stomach cancer 12 years earlier. Kappen was then moved to a subsidiary list which the detectives called the "Dead Pool." These individuals could be tested later on, by means of familial DNA. In the meantime, the task team continued tracking down other suspects.

In October 2001, there was another development in the case when a DNA profile was obtained from underwear worn by murder victim Sandra Newton. Detectives had always been divided as to whether Sandra had been killed by the same man who had killed Pauline and Geraldine. Now they had their answer. The same killer was responsible. Unfortunately, they still didn't know who he was.

Then, a short while after this latest breakthrough, someone had a brainwave. Since the murders had occurred in 1973, what were the chances that the killer had grown-up children? And since criminality is often passed from parents to children, was it possible that one or more of those children had a police record? Might their DNA be on file?

What at first seemed like a long shot soon delivered results when the killer's DNA profile was submitted to the NDNAD database and returned just over 100 potential matches. Those were eventually pared down to just one man, a convicted car thief by the name of Paul Kappen. Paul was the son of Joseph Kappen, whose name currently resided on the cold case team's "Dead Pool" list.

Joseph Kappen was now the number one suspect in the Saturday Night Strangler murders. But the evidence, though compelling, was not enough to close the case. What the investigators needed was a full DNA profile, to be matched against that of the known killer. In order to do that, the team would need to remove Kappen's body from its resting place in Goytre Cemetery on the outskirts of Port Talbot. On Christmas Eve 2001, DCI Bethell filed an application with the Home Office for an exhumation order.

That order would take eight months to be approved. In the interim, the team looked into the background of their suspect and found that he was a near exact match for the profile they'd been given. Joseph Kappen was a local man, born and raised in Port Talbot. He had a long history of arrests for petty crimes, dating back to 1953 when, at age 12, he was arrested for stealing money from gas meters. He'd been in and out of prison throughout his life and had seldom worked a regular job, preferring to live off the dole while doing odd jobs for cash. A six-footer and powerfully built, he often worked as a nightclub bouncer.

Kappen had married in 1962, when he was 20 years old and his bride, Christine, was just 17. He'd father three children during the tumultuous 18-year marriage. Although Christine described him as "tender and affectionate" during their early years, Kappen soon developed into a tyrant who terrorized his wife and children. The police were frequently called to his home to deal with domestic abuse issues but, as was common in those days, Kappen was never arrested for beating his wife. The profiler had also been correct about Kappen's "solitary" hobbies. He was obsessed with cars and often spent hours working on the junkers that littered his front lawn. He also raised song birds, tropical fish, and greyhounds. On one occasion, he had strangled a family pet in front of his children (both under 10 at the time) because he said that the dog was "too old." The children were understandably traumatized by the incident. Indeed, they grew up in terror of their violent and volatile father.

The police discovered something else about Kappen. He was apparently obsessed with teenaged girls and often boasted about his conquests to other bouncers at the clubs where he worked. And he wasn't above forcing himself on those who turned him down. In fact, the detectives found a number of reported incidents involving a man who closely matched Kappen's description. The most serious of these was a series of violent rapes that had occurred in the year before Sandra Newton was killed. In each of these cases, the rapist was described as six-foot tall, with bushy hair and a mustache. He was also said to smell of cigarette smoke (Kappen was a heavy smoker). Most of these victims were picked up while hitchhiking and driven to an isolated spot where their abductor demanded to know: "Are you a virgin?" He would then rape and sodomize the unfortunate girl before terrorizing her further by contemplating out loud whether he should kill her or not. It does not take a massive leap of faith to believe that this man was Joseph Kappen and that he soon after escalated from rape to murder.

On May 15, 2002, DCI Bethell eventually had his exhumation order, and a team of forensic archaeologists, forensic dentists, pathologists, and policemen descended on Goytre Cemetery. What started out a fine day had morphed into a violent thunder storm by the time they lifted Kappen's coffin out of the ground, something that those present took to be a portent of evil. Nonetheless, they soon had what they came for, several teeth and a section of femur bone, the likeliest sources of surviving DNA.

Three weeks later, the DNA results were back, confirming that Joseph Kappen was the Saturday Night Strangler. The revelation left the investigative team with mixed feelings. They had their man, but he would never stand before a judge and jury to answer for his terrible crimes. Joseph Kappen had gotten away with murder by dying before the law could catch up with him.

What Happens in Vegas

You would have thought that, after four failed marriages, Margaret would have given up on love. But no, the much-divorced blond still believed that Mr. Right was out there somewhere, and she believed she'd found him in millionaire property developer, Ron Rudin. Ron, too, had a patchy record in the marriage stakes. He'd acquired four ex-wives and a significant catalog of alimony obligations by the time his eye fell on the middle-aged, but still lithe, Margaret. That was during a service at the First Church of Religious Science in Las Vegas in 1987, the same church where the couple would marry later that year.

But this was no match made in heaven, as both parties were soon to discover. Ron was a philanderer and a heavy drinker; his bride was a neurotic and possessive woman who accused him of sleeping with everyone he so much as spoke to. Within months, the marriage was under strain, with Ron barring Margaret from his real estate office after one jealous outburst too many. She, in turn, told her sister that she wished her new husband would die. Margaret would eventually get her wish, but she would have to endure seven fractious years of marriage before it was granted to her.

On the morning of Tuesday, December 20, 1994, two of Ron Rudin's employees walked unto a Las Vegas police station and reported him missing. The workaholic realtor had failed to show up at his office on two consecutive days, and all attempts to reach him by phone had failed. The officer who took the report listened intently to the details and then picked up the phone to call the missing man's wife. Perhaps there was a rational explanation for his sudden disappearance. But Margaret nonchalantly informed the officer that what the employees had told him was correct, her husband had indeed disappeared. In fact, she'd been planning on filing a report herself and would be in later that afternoon to do so.

Margaret Rudin did eventually show up to make the missing person report, but her apparent lack of concern over her husband's whereabouts was an immediate red flag to the police. The following day, a couple of detectives paid a visit to the antique store she ran and asked if they could carry out a search of the couple's residence. Margaret said yes, but the detectives found nothing that might explain Ron's sudden disappearance.

That disappearance would remain a mystery until the night of January 21, 1995, when some fishermen discovered a human skull and several charred bones near Nelson's Landing, at the point where the Colorado River enters Lake Mohave. Dental records did the rest. It was Ron Rudin,, and he had been shot three times in the head. Three bullets, later removed from the skull cavity, would identify the murder weapon as a .22 caliber firearm. There was also another clue found at the makeshift cremation site: the scorched remains of a large antique steamer trunk. It appeared that Rudin had been brought to the area in the trunk, which had then been set alight with him inside. Since the trunk was heavy and bulky, at least two people would have been required to carry it. They would also have had to bring at least 50 gallons of gasoline with them. That was the amount it was estimated would have been required to cause such utter destruction of the corpse.

But who would have done such a thing? Who might have wanted Ron Rudin dead? Quite a few people, as it turned out. Rudin had made many enemies through his sometimes dodgy real estate deals. Several individuals also stood to gain from his $11 million estate after his death. One of those people, of course, was his wife, and from the very start, she was considered the main suspect. Her failure to report her husband missing; her lack of emotion when reporting the disappearance and also when she was told that his body had been found; her habit, even in the first days of the investigation, of referring to her husband in the past tense. None of these things amounted to evidence, but to experienced investigators, they were sign posts to be followed.

On the evening of January 27, 1995, detectives and a forensics team arrived at the Rudin residence armed with a search warrant. The search this time was far more thorough, turning up minute blood-spatters on the walls, the ceiling, an outlet cover, and an electrical switch plate. There were also bloodlike spatters on a box spring, found discarded in a nearby alleyway. That would be linked to the Rudin residence by a handyman, Augustine Lovato, who reported that Mrs. Rudin had hired him to do some work on January 21, the day after she reported her husband missing. According to Lovato, he had been told to clean up brownish stains on a carpet and was called back a few days later to entirely remodel the master bedroom, turning it into an office. While doing that work, he was required to remove items of furniture, including a box-spring and mattress. He was also asked to cut out a stained section of carpet and found a vile-smelling, brownish goo underneath it.

Other evidence soon began stacking up against the widow Rudin. Detectives learned that a close friend (and reputed lover) of hers, Yehuda Sharon, had rented a large passenger van from a car rental company in Las Vegas on the evening of December 19, 1994. Questioned about this, Sharon said that he had hired the truck in order to move stock from his business to Santa Fe Springs, California. He'd later decided against making the trip because of reports of adverse weather on route. Again, the police couldn't prove that he was lying, but it sounded suspicious. The van's odometer showed that it had covered 348 miles while in Sharon's possession. It might well have been used to transport the antique trunk with Ron Rudin's body inside. The timeline certainly matched.

And the police had, by now, established a link between the trunk and Margaret Rudin. An antiques dealer named Bruce Honabach claimed that he had sold just such a trunk to Margaret in the months before her husband was killed. According to Honabach, Margaret had told him on several occasions that she wished her husband would die. A similar claim came from a more unexpected source, Margaret's own sister, Donna Cantrell. According to Donna, Margaret had often confided her marital problems to her. On one occasion, she had asked why Margaret didn't just divorce him, as she had her previous four husbands. "He's not in very good health," Margaret had told her, "I think I'll wait."

So perhaps Margaret had grown tired of waiting and had decided to help Ron on his way into the afterlife. Investigators had by now formed a picture of how the murder might have occurred. They believed that Margaret had shot Ron in the head as he slept on the night of December 18. She had then recruited Yehuda Sharon to help her move the body, and Sharon had hired a van for that purpose on December 19. Ron had been loaded into the antique trunk and then driven to an area near Nelson's Landing where the trunk was doused with gasoline and then set alight with him inside. Ron had apparently feared just such an outcome. He'd inserted a clause in his will instructing his trustees to launch a full investigation should he die by violent means. He hadn't mentioned Margaret by name but, according to his attorney, that is exactly who he was afraid of.

The problem with the police case against Margaret Rudin was that much of the evidence was circumstantial or hearsay. Even the physical evidence wasn't as conclusive as it seemed. Ron Rudin was known to suffer from frequent nosebleeds. Any defense attorney worth his salt would use that to explain away the blood spatters found in the bedroom. As for the trunk that Bruce Honabach had supposedly sold to Margaret, Honabach didn't have an invoice, making his assertion close to useless. What the police really needed was the murder weapon. Nearly seven months after the murder, they found it.

On July 21, 1996, a man was scuba diving near Pyramid Island at Lake Mead, when he spotted an object wrapped in a plastic bag and secured by several rubber bands. That object turned out to be a .22 caliber Ruger handgun with a silencer still attached. When police ran the serial number through the ATF database, they were in for a surprise. The weapon was registered to Ron Rudin and had been reported missing by him in October 1988. According to the report he'd filed at the time, Ron had suspected his wife, Margaret, of stealing the gun. The couple had recently separated, and although they would later be reconciled, the weapon was never found. Until now. Subjected to

forensic testing, it turned out to be the gun that had taken Ron Rudin's
life.

On April 17, 1997, a Clark County grand jury handed down an
indictment against Margaret Rudin for the murder of her husband. A
warrant was then issued for her arrest, but when the police arrived to
serve it, they found that Margaret had fled. She would remain a
fugitive for over two years, changing her name and her appearance and
moving constantly, spending time in Illinois, Arizona, Mexico and
Massachusetts. During those years on the lam, her case appeared three
times on *America's Most Wanted*, and it was a tip generated by that
program that eventually led to her arrest. The former millionaire's wife
was found living in squalor with a retired firefighter in Revere,
Massachusetts. When officers arrived to take her into custody, she
reputedly said: "This is about Las Vegas, isn't it?"

Margaret Rudin appeared before the Eighth Judicial District Court in
Las Vegas on March 31, 2000, and entered not guilty pleas to the
charges against her. The case would be a controversial one with a less
than adequate performance by Rudin's defense attorney, Michael
Amador, and accusations that one of the jurors (who had wanted to
acquit Rudin) was bullied by the others into changing her vote.
Nonetheless, the verdict was guilty and the sentence was life in prison
with no possibility of parole for twenty years. A petition for a retrial
was later denied. Margaret Rudin will be 79 years old by the time she
can apply for early release.

Death by a Hundred Cuts

It started as a holiday romance. Michala Hall was a 24-year-old
divorcee enjoying a vacation at the beautiful Turkish resort of Bodrum
when she fell for a handsome 20-year-old waiter named Ensar Gol.
The two were virtually inseparable from that point on, and when
Michala eventually returned to England, they vowed to stay in touch.
Such promises, of course, are often made in the heat of passion, midst
exotic climes. They usually turn out to be empty once the cold reality
of everyday routine is re-established. But not in this case. Over the
next few years, Michala would spent all of her spare cash on travel to
Turkey, making at least three trips per year.

But, as Michala was soon to discover, there was another side to Ensar
Gol, a possessive, nasty side, a side that led him to be both verbally
and physically abusive. After one particularly violent confrontation,
during which Gol punched her in the face, Michala's mother urged her
to end the relationship. Michala, however, would hear none of it. She
was in love with Gol and thrilled when she found out that she was
pregnant with his child. In 2008, she gave birth to a daughter. Within a
year, they'd have a second child, a son this time.

Michala longed for Gol to move to England so that they could live together as a family. But Gol seemed reluctant to do so. Why would he, when he had such a great life in Turkey? There, he continued to live as a single man, seducing and sleeping with tourists. Michala was a handy source of cash, and he enjoyed the steady stream of gifts that she sent him. She'd even paid for his dental work. Yet, despite the two children they had together, Gol had no intention of building a life with her. In fact, while completing his national service in the Turkish military, he wrote to Michala and ended their relationship.

Michala was devastated at the news. In response, she traveled to Turkey where she picked up a relationship with an old flame, another Turkish man. But she soon regretted her action and flew back to Britain determined to win back Gol's love. She was over the moon when he contacted her in December 2010 and suggested that they patch things up. He even agreed to move to England and set up home with her and their children in Thame, Oxfordshire.

Thus it was that Michala returned to Turkey in March 2011, and married Gol in a traditional Turkish wedding. Immediately after, she got to work obtaining an immigration visa for her husband.

Married bliss, however, would be of short duration. Back in Turkey, Gol had heard a troubling rumor and had soon discovered that it was true. During their relationship break, his new bride had embarked on a fling with another man. To someone like Gol, fiercely jealous and from a culture where women are often regarded as possessions, it was the ultimate insult. The fact that Michala's one-time lover was a fellow Turk only made things worse. He called Michala and confronted her about the affair. Since it was pointless denying the allegations, she admitted them, although with the self-evident qualifier that he had broken up with her. She had been a single woman at the time. That did not sit well with Gol.

Over the weeks that followed, Gol became increasingly abusive towards his wife. The continental divide proved no impediment as he plagued Michala with phone calls and e-mails. He demanded that she account for her every movement and even took to monitoring her Facebook activity, deleting friends and posts of which he did not approve. Michala was often driven to despair by this long-distance abuse, even telling a friend that she was contemplating suicide. And yet, she still clung to her belief that if she could only get Gol to the UK, everything would be all right. In August 2011, her wish was granted. Gol's immigration visa had been approved.

Michala must have had mixed feelings about the reunion she had longed for. On the one hand, she still loved Gol and hoped to build a life with him. On the other, she was afraid of him, afraid of the barely contained rage that seemed to be bubbling just below the surface at all times. Still, she and Gol settled down to life in a house they shared with Michala's mother, Julie, and her husband, Mehmet Sahin, also a Turk. It did not take long for conflict to arise.

Gol was still furious at Michala's "betrayal" and never missed a chance to remind her of it, calling her a "whore" and a "slut." Within just two weeks of his arrival in the UK, the relationship had irrevocably broken down, and Michala ruefully informed her mother

that she had booked a plane ticket for Gol and that he would be
returning to Turkey.

Gol, however, would never make that flight. He was on his way to the
airport when he got a call from a tearful Michala, begging him not to
go. Given his open hostility towards his wife, it is surprising that he
agreed. The couple was reunited, although not in wedded bliss. Soon
the old pattern had been re-established, and now Gol had added
infidelity to his numerous sins against his wife. He began sleeping
with a local barmaid.

On September 2, 2011, just a week after he had agreed to remain in
England, Ensar Gol sent a curious and chilling message to a cousin on
Facebook. "I will cut them all," he wrote, "I will cut the mother-in-law
and the wife. All the English papers will talk about me tomorrow. The
crazy wolf Kurdish Turk who covered London in blood. The knife is
ready and you know I am handy with a knife." That same day, he
asked Julie's husband, Mehmet Sahin, what would happen to his
children if Julie and Michala were "gone." Knowing that Gol was fond
of such crazy talk, Mehmet laughed it off.

On the night of September 3, Michala was home with the children.
Also in the house were her mother Julie Sahin and a work colleague of
Julie's, 19-year-old Casey Wilson, who was a friend of both mother
and daughter. Mehmet Sahin was working a late shift at the pizza
restaurant where he was employed and Gol was out, having given his
wife no indication of his whereabouts or of the time he was likely to be
home. In fact, he was at a local bar, drinking heavily and then sneaking
off to have sex with his mistress.

By the time he did return home, considerably the worse for drink, it was two in the morning. Michala had already gone to bed, but Julie and Casey were still up, watching TV and talking. As Gol staggered through the door, he gave the two women a disdainful look and then walked past them without a word and entered the kitchen, where they heard him rummaging around. Then the women heard the sound of him working the latch on the child gate and then climbing the stairs. Moments later there were a series of thumps from the upper floor and a muffled scream.

Julie was immediately on her feet and was already halfway up the stairs when Casey followed. As Casey entered the darkened bedroom, she witnessed a chaotic scene. Michala was on the bed, thrashing around with arms and legs as she tried to free herself from her husband. Gol was on top of her and appeared to be punching her repeatedly. Then Julie joined the fight and tried to wrestle Gol off her daughter. She might have succeeded had she not slipped and fallen, at which point, Gol broke off his attack on Michala and diverted his attention to Julie. Now Casey became involved, trying to pull Gol away from her friends. In response, he spun around and punched her in the neck. At least, she thought it was a punch until a jagged shard of pain told her that she had been cut. It was then that she appreciated the true horror of the situation. Gol had a knife, and as she collapsed to the floor, he was on her. It took all of her will, all of her strength, to hold him off. Even so, she suffered several deep wounds before she managed to break free.

Casey staggered to her feet and out of the room, down the stairs and out into the night, terrified that Gol might come after her. Once she was sure that he wasn't following, she got out her cellphone and dialed 999 with trembling fingers. She then waited on the street, holding a hand to her neck wound in an attempt to stem the flow of blood.

Minutes passed, minutes that felt like hours. Then she heard the wail of sirens and an ambulance raced past her. Already groggy from loss of blood, she followed.

Back at the house, Casey peered past the paramedics and saw Julie lying in a fetal position at the foot of the stairs, her clothing soaked in blood. One of the medics was working on her, but then he stood up and shook his head. Casey was later taken to John Radcliffe Hospital in Oxford, where surgeons operated for two hours to stitch up her multiple knife wounds. She had been lucky. The blade had come within millimeters of her jugular.

While all of this was going on, another drama had been playing itself out. After murdering his wife and mother-in-law, Ensar Gol had picked up his three-year-old daughter. The little girl had been lying in bed beside her mother during the brutal attack. Now Gol would subject her to further trauma. Police officers soon picked him up on CCTV, aimlessly wandering the streets in his bloodstained clothes, the kitchen knife in one hand, dripping blood, the terrified little girl straddling his other hip. For fear that he might harm the child, police officers were forced to hang back. It was only after Gol entered the pizza restaurant where Mehmet Sahin was working and handed the little girl over to him, that officers were able to move in and arrest Gol. At the time, Gol was on the phone to his family in Turkey, telling them what he'd done. He seemed more concerned about his bloodied clothing than about the two murders he'd committed.

Once in custody, Ensar Gol offered a fanciful story, insisting that Michala had attacked him and that he had been forced to defend himself. At trial, he told a different explanation for the murders, saying that he had felt trapped in the relationship and that his mother-in-law's dislike for him, and her constant sniping had pushed him over the edge.

Did any of these reasons provide justification for the 100 knife wounds he had inflicted on his three victims? The jury certainly didn't think so. It took them just two-and-a-half hours to find Gol guilty of two counts of murder and one of attempted murder. The judge then passed sentence of 36 years for each of the murders and 12 years for the attempt on Casey Wright's life. Gol will have to serve at least 30 years before he is eligible for parole. Not that it appeared to bother the killer. He was led from the courtroom grinning broadly, pointing at himself with two fingers and mouthing the words: "Me, me, me".

Desperado

He called himself Tex McCord, a name he'd borrowed from a long-dead western outlaw; he said that he was from Texas, that his family owned a ranch there and that he had spent his whole life around steers and broncos. In reality, the man applying for a job at the Whitetail Ranch near Ovando, Montana, was none of these things. His real name was Roger Caryl and he was from Mount Zion, Illinois. Just a few short months earlier, he'd been a set-upon high school kid, a regular target for bullies. The closest he'd ever come to being a cowboy was when he'd donned a Stetson and a sheriff's badge for his school's Fall Festival.

Still, John Miller was shorthanded and he was hiring. "Tex" talked a good game, and so Miller gave him a job on the spot. He'd soon have cause to regret that decision. To call Tex inept would have been a vast understatement of the word. He could ride a pony but beyond that lacked even the most basic of cowhand skills. He was also a braggart who claimed to have served in Vietnam with the U.S. Marines. Since his tender age made those assertions an obvious falsehood, he soon got into conflict with another ranch hand, 42-year-old Sam Akins, who

called him out as a liar. Aside from that, Tex soon made himself
known to law enforcement in Ovando. On at least three occasions, he
was picked up for driving under the influence. Paying scant attention
to the warnings handed out by local deputies, he then went on yet
another bender and wrecked his employer's truck.

By October 1973, John Miller had taken just about as much as he was
going to take. The only thing that prevented him from firing Tex on
the spot was that they were at the tail-end of the tourist season.
Whitetail was a "dude ranch" which catered to city folk wanting to
come and play cowboy for a few days. Business generally dipped off
in the winter months, and once it did, Miller planned on giving Tex his
marching orders. But then, Tex forced his hand by shooting one of his
dogs. Tex claimed that the animal had attacked him, but Miller knew
that that wasn't true. He instructed Tex to bury the dog and to come
and see him at the ranch house the next morning.

Tex McCord probably knew what was coming. The wannabe cowboy
was about to be fired and kicked off the only ranch he'd ever lived on.
His dream of the cowboy life was about to come to an end. Although
he would later try to blame what happened on drugs and alcohol, there
can be little doubt that anger over his imminent dismissal played its
part.

Whatever the reason, McCord went back to the bunkhouse, picked up
a shotgun and gunned down Sam Akins and his 18-year-old son,
Stephen. He then strode across to the ranch house carrying the shotgun
and with a pistol and two knives tucked into his belt. John Miller was
in the kitchen, standing at the table and feeding his baby daughter
when McCord entered. Also present were Miller's wife, Roberta, and

the cook, 62-year-old Ruby Judd. Fourteen-year-old Steve Foundation, who also lived at the ranch, was in an upstairs room and hid in a closet once the shooting started.

John Miller took the first shotgun blast. Aware of what was coming, Miller had placed the baby on the table and raised his hands in an effort to placate McCord. "I have a few hellos for you, and here's one from Tex McCord," Tex apparently told him. Then he pulled the trigger, hitting the young rancher full in the chest. McCord then fired at Roberta Miller but missed as she ducked under the table. That gave Ruby Judd the chance to make a grab for the gun. But the elderly woman was no match for McCord. He soon wrestled the weapon free and then shot her dead before walking casually from the kitchen, leaving Roberta cowering under the table. He then threw his gear into a pickup and drove away.

By the following morning, a massive manhunt was underway for Tex McCord, now sought for four murders. The authorities were convinced that they would make a quick arrest. The terrain around Ovando was rugged, and the "greenhorn" Tex was not equipped to live in the mountains. That meant that he'd probably try to drive out of the area. With roadblocks stretching north-south from U.S. 12 to Montana 200, and hundreds of officers and volunteers scouring the brush, it seemed that an arrest was imminent.

But McCord proved far more resourceful than the police were giving him credit for. Despite the use of spotter planes and tracking dogs, he slipped the dragnet. Soon the local cops were forced to turn to the FBI for help, and Tex made it onto the *Ten Most Wanted List*. By now, his legend was growing. The story was that he had used his skills as an

Eagle Scout to cross the Rockies to freedom, without supplies and armed only with a Buck knife. Officially, he was now being described as "armed and very dangerous." It was said that he was a skilled outdoorsman and a crack shot who could "blow a man's head off at 500 yards." Such was the fear his reputation garnered that when he was supposedly spotted near Helena, that city's hotels quickly filled up with ranchers who were afraid to stay on their farms.

The truth, of course, was far removed from these stories. Roger Caryl wasn't some desperado, he was a frightened teenager. Caryl had been born in Japan while his father was serving in the military there, and raised on a smallholding in rural Illinois. At school, he'd been an average student who had the occasional disciplinary problem, but nothing that warranted more than a temporary suspension. From an early age, he'd showed a fascination with the Old West, devouring books on cowboys and gunfighters. He also liked to wear western clothes and cowboy boots, and tried to talk with a Texan drawl. That, unsurprisingly, made him a target for bullies who enjoyed mussing his hair, knocking his books from his hands and kicking his schoolbag down the stairs. All of this led to Caryl becoming isolated from his peers.

And the situation at home was barely much better. Caryl's parents appear to have favored an "uninvolved" parenting style, leading to him becoming increasingly withdrawn and uncommunicative. He retreated instead to the novels of Louis L'Amour and Zane Grey and to books about the Old West and the Confederacy. A few weeks after graduation, Roger told his father that he was going on a camping trip and instead hit the road west, ending up at the Whitetail Ranch. The next time his parents heard of their son was when FBI agents knocked on their door and informed them that he was a suspect in four murders.

Roger Caryl a.k.a. Tex McCord was eventually captured in February of 1974 in Ft. Lauderdale, Florida. Someone had recognized him from a wanted poster and tipped off the police. At his trial, he entered a plea of not guilty by reason of insanity. According to Caryl's testimony he'd started worrying that he was going to be fired on the night before the shootings. He had sought solace in the bottle and was drunk by the time Sam and Stephen Akins arrived at the bunkhouse in the company of a "long-haired" man. This man, according to Caryl, gave him a "red pill" which he swallowed. He then blacked out and only regained his senses a couple of days later, when he woke up in a motel room. He could remember nothing that happened during those lost days, he said. He specifically had no recollection of the shootings.

This "selective amnesia" defense is, of course, a popular one with criminals, even if it seldom works. Nonetheless, Caryl was extensively examined by a team of psychologists at the Warm Springs State Hospital, the tests lasting for a period of four weeks. The doctors found no evidence of mental disorder but did find that Caryl was a "socially maladjusted passive-aggressive with a propensity for episodic excessive drinking and drug abuse." Much of this, the report suggested, was rooted in his childhood. It did not amount to an excuse for quadruple homicide.

Roger Caryl was found guilty on two counts of murder and sentenced to consecutive life terms, with parole eligibility in 25 years. The sentences related to the killings of John Miller and Ruby Judd. Oddly, Caryl was never charged with the murders of Samuel and Stephen Akins.

In 2004, The Helena Independent Record reported that Roger Caryl
was living in a prison pre-release program in Butte, Montana. In 2006,
he was transferred to a similar low-security program in Muskogee,
Oklahoma. He has since been granted full parole, with his current
whereabouts unknown.

In the end, Roger Caryl's boyhood dream of becoming a desperado out
of one of his favorite Western novels, was realized. Four innocent
people and their families had paid a terrible price as a consequence.

To Kill and Kill Again

Leigh Robinson had a problem with women. If ever you needed validation of that statement, you only had to observe Robinson's behavior around his circle of male acquaintances compared to the way he treated the women in his life. With his male friends, Robinson was the typical party guy, the life of any gathering. With women, it was "my way or the highway." And with Leigh Robinson, the "highway" often amounted to physical violence. Sometimes it even amounted to death.

Robinson's misogynistic leanings can perhaps be traced back to his relationship with his mother, or rather to their lack of a relationship. Robinson's parents had divorced when he was just four years old, and although his mother, Gwen, retained custody, she was a wholly unfit parent, shunting him from one relative to another while she pursued her party lifestyle. That left the boy with unresolved issues which would manifest in acts of petty criminality as he grew older. At thirteen, he was expelled from school, never to return. Later, he'd enlist in the army, although military discipline was a poor fit for the criminally inclined Robinson. After his discharge, he would return to the Melbourne suburb of Chadstone where he had grown up. There, he moved in with an old army mate, Ricky Foster.

Robinson was now 18 years old, tall and handsome with an easy line of chat that made him apparently irresistible to women. Before long he had attracted the attention of Valerie Dunn, a pretty 17-year-old who worked as a store clerk and lived four doors down from the Foster residence. They started dating, with Robinson even getting a job alongside Valerie's father, Harold, in his carpeting business. However, the rest of the family kept Robinson at arm's length, mainly because of his loud, boastful persona. They were also aware of his reputation as a juvenile delinquent. By then, Robinson was already well-known to local law enforcement as a petty thief and vandal.

Before long, Valerie had also picked up on her family's attitude towards Robinson. Leigh could be polite and charming when things were going his way, but the moment he perceived a slight, the moment you disagreed with him, he changed. Valerie had already endured threats and actual violence. On more than one occasion, she'd been choked and manhandled. Eventually, she decided that enough was enough. She told Leigh that it was over. A short time later, she began dating a former boyfriend, Des Grewar.

You can only imagine Robinson's reaction. Valerie and Des were stalked and threatened. On one occasion, Valerie was even abducted and held for several hours. She was only released after the police arrived with Valerie's father who managed to talk Robinson into releasing her. Amazingly, no charges were pressed in connection with this incident. Robinson even kept his job with Harold Dunn. That would turn out to be a tragic mistake.

On June 8, 1968, Robinson was working with Harold at a location in central Melbourne. During the afternoon, Harold sent him to drop off some supplies at another work site. Robinson was supposed to return after making that delivery. Instead, he drove to the Dunn residence where Des Grewar was visiting Valerie.

After entering the home, Robinson insisted on talking to Valerie alone in the kitchen. She agreed to talk to him but rebuffed his invitation to go with him to a local tenpin bowling alley. This apparently infuriated Robinson. Before Valerie even knew what was happening, he snatched up a kitchen knife and plunged it into her side. Then as the young woman slid to the floor, he was on her, driving the blade repeatedly into her back, inflicting 14 deep wounds. When Des Grewar came to his girlfriend's aid, he, too, was attacked, suffering two serious stab wounds. He would ultimately survive. Valerie Dunn would not.

Robinson was arrested later that night after he handed himself over at the Cranbourne police station. Despite overwhelming evidence against him, he insisted that he was innocent, offering the ludicrous story that he had arrived at the Dunn residence to find Valerie stabbed and bleeding on the ground. He was still telling that fanciful tale when he went on trial in November 1968. However, the evidence of Des Grewar was enough to prove that he was lying. Robinson was found guilty and, in Australia at that time, there could be only one sanction. He was sentenced to death.

By rights, Robinson should have died on the gallows at Pentonville Prison. But there were political moves afoot at that time that would work to his advantage. Public opposition to capital punishment was growing, and there had been several abolitionist marches and protests. Robinson also cut a sympathetic figure, perceived by the public as a lovelorn young man who had allowed his passion to get the better of him. His case, therefore, became a political landmine for Victoria state governor, Rohan Delacombe, to deal with. At a meeting of the state Cabinet six months after Robinson's trial, it was decided to commute his sentence to 30 years' hard labor. Robinson served just 15 years before being paroled in 1983.

After his release, Robinson started a relationship with a woman named Gina, who he had met while serving his prison sentence. Gina had been a regular visitor to Pentonville where she taught prisoners how to make soft toys. Robinson had made such an impression on her that she allowed him to move into her home with her five children. There, he quickly assumed the role of stepfather and was, to outside eyes at least, a reformed character. The truth was somewhat different. In 1991, Robinson was back inside on a charge of receiving stolen goods. He served two years before being released again. Thereafter, he started sexually assaulting his teenaged stepdaughters.

The truth of those assaults would remain hidden until 1994, when one of the girls was old enough to leave home and subsequently reported the rapes and assaults to the police. Robinson was duly tried and convicted, drawing a five-year sentence. Even then, Gina (who had married Robinson the previous year) refused to believe that he was guilty. She sided with him against her own daughters.

Such was the hold that Robinson appeared to have on women. Shortly after his release on the rape charges, another young woman was drawn into his toxic sphere of influence. Like Valerie Dunn, she would pay dearly for her infatuation.

Tracey Greenbury was born six years after Leigh Robinson began his sentence for murdering Valerie Dunn; she was in primary school at the time he walked free. Yet Tracey, 33 years old at the time that she met the 60-year-old Robinson, was inexplicably drawn to him. Like Gina, Tracey had met Robinson through a prison connection. In Tracey's case, it was through her brother Jeffrey who was serving a prison term for murder when he met Robinson. After both men had been released, Jeffrey invited Robinson to a barbeque at his house, and it was there that Robinson first encountered Tracey. Before long they were dating.

But Tracey soon learned, as had so many women before her, that Leigh Robinson was a difficult man to get along with. He could be charming, sure, but he was also quick to anger and just as quick to physical violence. On several occasions, Tracey was assaulted and threatened. Matters eventually came to ahead on April 27, 2008, when Robinson held a gun to her head and told her that he was going to shoot her.

Tracey spent that night at her parents' house, but the following day, April 28, she returned to her own home. She'd barely arrived when Robinson pulled up in his car. When he got out, he was holding a sawn-off shotgun. Tracey tried to run and actually succeeded in evading Robinson and fleeing to a neighbor's house. Perhaps she thought that the proximity of another person would dissuade Robinson from doing anything stupid, but she was wrong. As she lay cowering on the floor in her neighbor's hallway, Robinson pressed the gun barrel to the side of her head. Then, with the terrified neighbor standing just a couple of feet away, he pulled the trigger, ending the life of the woman he professed to love.

Robinson would spend the next few days on the run, although it appeared more like a farewell tour than an actual attempt to avoid capture. During that time, he visited friends and family before eventually surrendering to the police. At his subsequent trial, he provoked outrage with his cavalier attitude, laughing and waving to friends in the gallery while evidence of the brutal murder was being presented.

In many ways, the Tracey Greenbury trial echoed that for the murder of Valerie Dunn decades earlier. Robinson again pled not guilty, this time claiming that he had only meant to frighten Tracey and that the gun had discharged accidentally. His frankly ridiculous defense was again eviscerated by the prosecution and rejected by the jury. Found guilty of murder, Robinson was sentenced to life in prison without the possibility of parole.

Choke Hold

The thing that people remember most about Dana Laskowski was her love for children. The 36-year-old single mother absolutely doted on her triplets and yet still had the time and energy to offer her services as a babysitter in Puyallup, Washington, a quite suburb of Tacoma. And she was much in demand, not just because of her instinctive rapport with kids, but also because she could always be relied on. So when she failed to show up for one of her regular babysitting jobs on the morning of August 31, 2001, her employer was immediately concerned. After making several calls to Dana and getting no reply, the woman phoned the police and asked them to check in on her.

A patrol officer was directed to the address and arrived to find the house securely locked, with no sign of activity from within. After knocking and getting no response, the officer looped around to the rear of the property and entered through a back door which stood ajar. It wasn't long before he found Dana, lying on the couch, a pillow under her head and a blanket pulled over the lower half of her body. There was blood on her nose and mouth and her face had the flushed appearance of someone who had been asphyxiated. After checking for a pulse and finding none, the officer called it in.

Investigators who arrived at Dana Laskowski's home that morning noted a couple of things. Firstly, there was no evidence of a forced entry; second, despite the violent way in which the victim had died, there was very little sign of a struggle. Dana had been strangled to death, and judging by a patch of blood on the carpet, the murder had happened right in front of the couch where she'd been found. The killer had then picked her up, laid her out on the couch, placed a pillow under her head and covered her with a blanket. In the opinion of detectives, that indicated remorse on the part of the killer. That, in turn, pointed to someone who had known Dana. As the police were about to discover, there were no shortage of suspects.

The first of those was a cable guy by the name of Paco McKenna who had recently done some work at Dana's house and had apparently become obsessed with her. Dana had complained to friends that he'd been stalking her, calling her at all hours of the day and night, leaving flowers and poems on her doorstep, even hanging around outside her house. Had McKenna become frustrated by Dana's rejection of him? Had he snapped and strangled her? The police certainly thought it was a possibility, but McKenna had an alibi, and a search of his house and car turned up nothing incriminating. He admitted to calling Dana but denied stalking her. "I thought she was attractive and asked her for a date," he said. "If that's a crime, then I confess."

McKenna, though, wasn't the only man in Dana's life. She had been dating a man named Miles Liburn who lived just across the border in Vancouver, Canada. According to those who knew the couple, Miles was besotted with Dana while her feelings for him were less intense. In fact, Dana had confessed to a friend that she had already cheated on Miles. She'd had a one-night stand with his close friend, Jace Harwick. That, of course, made both men viable suspects, but again the police were frustrated when their respective alibis checked out.

And then there was Shane Littsky, Dana's ex-husband and the father of her triplets. Shane was, by all accounts, still in love with his ex-wife and jealous of the new men in her life. He and Dana clashed often over the issue, with Shane complaining that he didn't want his children interacting with men he didn't know. But Shane, too, had a seemingly watertight alibi. He'd had his kids that weekend and had taken them camping, along with a group of friends. He'd been three hundred miles away at the time of the murder.

Ten days after her tragic death, Dana Laskowski was laid to rest. As is often the case in murder inquiries there were several undercover cops at the service, surreptitiously observing the mourners. There was also a police photographer outside the church, photographing the license plates of the cars parked there. It was he who brought an interesting clue to investigators, reporting that the windshield of Shane Littsky's car was covered in bugs. It had recently been driven for some distance.

This snippet of information sent detectives scurrying to re-examine Shane Littsky's alibi. According to him, he'd been camping at Bank's Lake, a 3-hour drive from his ex-wife's residence, on the night of the murder. Was it possible that he'd waited until everyone at the campsite was asleep, then snuck away and driven to Dana's house, committed the murder and then driven back? Detectives drove the route and figured out that it could be done. However, their subsequent efforts to place Littsky on I-90 that night, via traffic cameras and gas stations, all failed. In any case, a profile of the suspect, drawn up by an FBI expert, was now pushing the investigation in a different direction.

According to the FBI profiler, the person who had killed Dana Laskowski had not arrived at her house with the intention of committing murder. "This was a situation that got out of control," he said. "It happened on the spur of the moment." That ruled out Shane Littsky's long, moonlight drive.

Where exactly did that leave the investigation? With a few disparate threads of circumstantial evidence and no forensics to back them up. The killer had known Dana, had arrived at her house with no intent to kill, and had more than likely murdered her during an altercation. The only other thing that they were sure of was that the killer was a powerful person. So much pressure had been applied to Dana's throat that her windpipe had been crushed.

Two years had now passed, and the police were no closer to solving Dana Laskowski's murder than they had been on the morning they'd found her brutalized body. But then detectives became aware of an aspect of Dana's life that they previously had been unaware of. It appeared that Dana's love of children was not confined to toddlers. She was also a "den mother" of sorts to a group of disaffected teens who hung around in local parks. Dubbed the "Park Rats," this group included runaways, drug addicts and some petty criminals who Dana invited into her home. At times, she even left her door unlocked so that they could get in while she wasn't around to shower or to do their laundry. She had apparently been particularly fond of one of the group, a 16-year-old named Aba Kopf who was a perpetual runaway and also a drug user.

Kopf was tracked down and brought in for questioning. She denied knowing anything about Dana's murder but was quick to offer up a potential suspect, an 18-year-old named Levi Spire. Spire was well-known to the police. He was a petty criminal and small-time drug dealer with a long rap sheet. He was also a muscular six-footer. Someone, in other words, who could easily have overpowered Dana Laskowski.

But finding Spire would prove more difficult than the police had anticipated. He appeared to have dropped out of sight. Instead, detectives tracked down one of his known associates, a youth named Max Brindley who was currently in the county lockup awaiting trial on drugs offenses. Brindley chuckled when the officers mentioned Spire as a potential murder suspect. "That wasn't Levi," he said. "Everyone knows who killed Dana." He then offered up a name, which the detectives immediately dismissed.

Like Max Brindley and Levi Spires, Emily Lauenborg was well-known to the police. She was one of the "Park Rats," a scrawny 17-year-old with a record for shoplifting, theft, and drug possession. But the suggestion that she might have killed Dana Laskowski was ludicrous. Lauenborg stood just 5-foot-2 and she was scrawny, weighing in at barely 115 pounds. There was no way that she could have inflicted the kind of injuries found on Dana's body. Or could she?

Looking deeper into Lauenborg's background, detectives discovered that she went by the nickname "The Mutant" because of her unusual strength. She had once been a weightlifting champion, and she was known to challenge boys much bigger than her to wrestling bouts which she usually won. She also appeared to have a temper. Perhaps she was not such an unlikely suspect after all.

In March 2003, Puyallup detectives brought Emily Lauenborg in for questioning and immediately walked into a brick wall. She flatly denied having anything to do with the murder and challenged the investigators to prove otherwise. With no physical evidence linking her to the crime, they were forced to let her go. Emily was tough, and they doubted they'd break her down under interrogation. A more likely path to the truth was Aba Kopf.

The police had since learned something about the relationship between Kopf and Lauenborg. The two of them were close. So close, in fact, that they had a well-rehearsed double act where they'd talk themselves into a boy's house and Aba would then distract him and his friends with a strip show while Emily robbed the place. They also resorted to simple break-ins at times. One of their frequent victims was Dana Laskowski.

Aba Kopf was brought in for a second round of questioning and, under pressure from the police, she soon folded, implicating her friend in Dana Laskowski's death. According to Kopf, she and Lauenborg had arrived at Dana's house that night to ask her for money to buy drugs. Dana, however, had refused them and had then asked them to leave after Lauenborg started to become abusive. She then pushed Lauenborg towards the door, but that was a mistake. Emily had turned on her, got her in a choke hold and started applying pressure, keeping it up until Dana went limp and collapsed to the floor. According to Kopf, she had fled the house at that point. It was Lauenborg who had dragged Dana's body onto the couch and arranged it so that it looked like she was asleep. She'd then robbed the place before leaving.

Confronted with her friend's statement, Emily Lauenborg continued to protest her innocence. But the evidence quickly started stacking up against her. She had hardly been discreet about the murder, boasting to several friends about it. The police also found several incriminating items at her home, including a journal in which she had recorded: "I wish I could kill Aba the way I killed Dana." There was also a handwritten "Bucket List." At #9 she had listed: "Kill someone and get away with it."

Neither of those were conclusive evidence of murder. There were, however, items in Lauenborg's possession which proved, at the very least, that she had robbed Dana Laskowski. One of those items, a black blouse, looked oddly familiar to the investigators. Then they revisited old surveillance photographs and realized why. Emily had worn the stolen blouse to her victim's funeral. That pointed to an incredibly cold and callous person.

With Aba Kopf agreeing to testify against her friend at trial, the case against Emily Lauenborg looked like a slam dunk. Yet Lauenborg had a few things going for her. One was her age; the other was the lack of premeditation. The prosecution also knew that her defense team would likely argue that her intention had not been to kill but to subdue. With this in mind, the D.A. offered Lauenborg a deal, allowing her to plead to a reduced charge of first-degree manslaughter. She would spend just six years in prison before her release in 2007. Aba Kopf, who had stood by and done nothing while her friend was murdered before her eyes, faced no charges at all.

Every Contact Leaves a Trace

The city of Port Hueneme, California, is a small beach community in Ventura County, some 60 miles north of Los Angeles. It is a good place to live and raise a family, with beautiful year-round weather and some excellent schools, both in the city itself and in nearby Oxnard. Crime is low, and violent crime, particularly murder, is a rarity. Or at least it was until the summer of 1993 when the city experienced three brutal homicides in the space of just two months.

The first of those involved a 32-year-old single mother named Norma Garcia Rodriguez. On the morning of June 2, 1993, a Ventura County 911 operator received a frantic call from a man named Anthony Rodriguez. According to Rodriguez, he had arrived at the home of his estranged wife to pick up his two sons. After knocking for several minutes, his sons had opened the door for him, and he'd then entered the home and found his wife lying dead on the lounge floor.

Units were quickly dispatched to the modest two-bedroom home on East B Street, where they found a distraught Rodriguez comforting his

sons Anthony Jr. and Austin. The body still lay where Rodriguez had
found it, and the officers could immediately see that this was no
ordinary murder. Norma Rodriguez's entire head was encased in silver
duct tape. Crime scene investigators would later determine that 20 feet
of the stuff had been used and that the killer had wrapped it around his
victim's head 14 times either while she was unconscious or already
dead. Norma had also been strangled. Either way, she'd died of
asphyxiation.

From early on in the investigation, detectives were convinced that
there was a personal motive to the crime. There was no sign of forced
entry or of a struggle, meaning that Norma had most likely let her
killer into the house and had been taken completely by surprise when
he turned on her. There was also no evidence of sexual assault; neither
had anything been stolen from the residence. A forensic psychologist
suggested that the bizarre nature of the crime indicated that the killer
had not wanted to see Norma's face. Possibly he felt a deep sense of
guilt over what he had done to her. Yes, the clues certainly pointed to
someone within the victim's inner circle. But who?

The obvious suspect was Anthony Rodriguez, Norma's estranged
husband. According to Rodriguez, he'd taken older son Anthony to a
baseball game the previous day while Austin had stayed behind with
his mother. He'd dropped the boy off at around 9 a.m. but had not
come inside and had driven directly home. Anthony Jr. confirmed this.
He said that he had found the house locked and in darkness. Not
wanting to wake his mother by knocking, he had gone around to the
bedroom that he shared with his younger brother and had climbed
through the window. Austin had already been in bed and had told
Anthony that their mom was "sleeping" and that she had "something
on her face." Anthony had told him to go to sleep, and the boys had

soon drifted off, remaining in bed until their father's knocking had
woken them the next morning.

This testimony seemed to suggest that Norma was already dead by the
time Anthony Jr. got home and thus cleared his father. Rodriguez Sr.,
in any case, agreed to a polygraph and passed. It seemed he was in the
clear.

Attention next turned to a man named Dennis Garza, who Norma had
recently been dating. Garza was known to have a somewhat explosive
temper and, according to friends, he and Norma had fought often.
Recently, he had called off the relationship to return to an old flame.
Norma had apparently been devastated. Had they clashed over the
break-up? Had things gotten out of hand? Apparently not. Garza had a
cast-iron alibi and he also passed a polygraph. Frustratingly, the police
were back to square one.

But not for long. Investigators soon uncovered two very interesting
snippets of information. The first involved a friend and work colleague
of Norma's named Beatrice. Beatrice had been having an extra-marital
affair and had roped in Norma as a confidant. In fact, Norma had given
Beatrice a set of keys to her house so that Beatrice could use the
residence for her illicit trysts. Had Beatrice's husband found out? Had
he killed Norma in revenge? The man was brought in for questioning
but denied involvement in the murder. It was also clear to investigators
that he had been oblivious to his wife's affair. That, in turn, removed
any motive he might have had for murder.

The second clue had to do with a missing set of keys. On the day prior to her death, Norma had hosted a barbeque for friends and co-workers from the Oxnard K-Mart where she worked as an assistant manager. At one point, she had asked her guests to help her look for her house keys which she claimed to have lost. Despite their efforts, the keys had never been found. Had someone at the barbeque pocketed them with the intention of returning later to sneak into the house? Who among Norma's friends might have done such a thing? Investigators believed that the answer might lie with Norma's younger son, Austin, who had been in the house when his mother was killed.

Questioning a four-year-old about a murder is a delicate matter. The boy was undoubtedly confused over what had happened and might well be suffering some form of post-traumatic stress. Nonetheless, Austin turned out to be a more than adequate witness. He said that there had been a man in their house, that he had heard his mother scream, and that the man had then put tape over his mother's mouth. Asked if he knew the man, the little boy nodded. Then he offered up a name: "Warren."

Warren turned out to be Warren Mackey, a 39-year-old co-worker of Norma Rodriguez. Looking into his background, investigators discovered that he did not have a police record, that he'd worked with Norma for two years, and that colleagues described him as quiet and introverted. They also found out that he had attended Norma's barbeque the previous day and that he appeared to have a crush on her. Norma's friends claimed that he frequently pestered her to go out with him and that her refusals did nothing to put him off. He had apparently been distraught at her death but had not attended the funeral. That contrast seemed suspicious.

Mackey, of course, denied involvement in the murder, offered an alibi (which checked out) and agreed to take a polygraph (which he passed). Detectives were beginning to think that young Austin had been mistaken, and those suspicions grew when the boy gave them another name, Clive, who turned out to be another of his mother's co-workers. According to Austin's latest account, it was Clive and not Warren who had struggled with his mother.

Clive was Clive Dalton, an outgoing and, it appeared, universally liked K-Mart employee. But he was hiding a shocking secret from his colleagues. Currently, he was a suspect in a rape case. He also seemed extremely nervous when detectives questioned him. That demeanor, coupled with his arrest record, shifted him to the top of the suspect list for a while. But Dalton was able to account for his whereabouts on the night of the murder and also passed the obligatory lie detector test.

To the frustration of the Port Hueneme police, all of their main suspects had now been questioned and eliminated from the inquiry. They still had DNA, obtained from under the victim's fingernails and from the duct tape, but in 1993, the technology was in its infancy and they could not extract a viable sample. Then, as the Rodriguez case languished, the city was rocked by two extremely violent homicides in the space of a month.

The first victim was Beatrice Bellis, an 87-year-old woman who was both deaf and mute. She was raped and stabbed to death inside her one-bedroom apartment within a care facility for the elderly. Then, firefighters were called to a burning condominium in Outlook Cove and found the body of 44-year-old Cynthia Burger inside. She had been raped and strangled, and the killer had apparently started the fire in an effort to destroy evidence.

Were these killings connected to the murder of Norma Rodriguez? The police didn't think so. The M.O.s and victim profiles were just too different. Still, that didn't stop the local media from blaring out that there was a serial killer loose on the streets of Port Hueneme. For a time, the quiet seaside town went into a state of virtual lockdown.

Ten years passed during which the murder of Norma Rodriguez (and those of the other two victims) ground to a halt and eventually went cold. To most observers, it appeared that the killer or killers had gotten away with murder. But not to the Port Hueneme police. They remained committed to solving the murders, and in 2003, the advances in DNA technology allowed them to do just that. The Bellis murder turned out to be the handiwork of one Michael Schultz, who had been working as a handyman in the complex where his victim had lived. Ricardo Villa, an auto mechanic, was linked to the murder of Cynthia Burger. Both of the killers still lived in the area and were soon under arrest. Both were subsequently convicted and sentenced to death.

The Rodriguez murder, however, was more complicated. Norma had not been raped, and so there was no semen to extract a DNA sample from. All the police lab had was fingernail clippings and a length of duct tape. Nonetheless, they did manage to extract a profile and to run it against the original suspects in the case. They soon had a match… to Warren Mackey, Norma's oft-jilted suitor.

But what did the DNA match tell them, really? Warren and Norma worked together and he'd been a guest in her house the day before her death. There was ample opportunity for DNA to pass innocently between them. Perhaps, but DNA on the duct tape was another matter. That could only have been left behind by the killer.

Mackey was brought in for what he thought was a routine, follow-up interview. Told that his DNA had been found on Norma, he appeared stunned. That couldn't be, he protested, because he and Norma had never had sex. Apparently, he was under the impression that DNA is only passed during sexual contact. That is wrong, of course. To quote the forensic investigator's credo: "Every contact leaves a trace."

Warren Mackey was arrested and charged with first-degree murder. Facing the prospect of the death penalty if found guilty, he asked for a deal, pleading guilty to second-degree murder and accepting a jail term of 15 years to life.

Repeat Offender

Albert Goozee

On a pleasant June day in 1956, a motorist was driving his car through
Bignall Wood, an area of the New Forest in southeast Dorset, England.
He'd just turned onto a quiet, tree-lined lane when he spotted another
vehicle, a black Wolseley, by the side of the road. There was a man
slumped over the hood of the vehicle. He appeared to be injured.

Assuming that the man had been involved in a car accident, the
motorist pulled over. He could see right away that his initial
impression had been correct. The man was definitely hurt. In fact,
there was blood seeping from an apparent stomach wound into his
shirt. "There's been a fight," he rasped as the motorist approached.
"I've put the knife in." He then went on to explain that he had killed
his landlady and her daughter after they had attacked him. He also
urged the motorist to follow him into the woods so that he could show
him where the bodies were. Perhaps wisely, the man decided to go for
the police instead.

Police officers were soon on the scene and found the injured man still waiting, still clutching his hand to his stomach wound. Asked for his name, the man said that he was Albert William Goozee. He then told the officers that there had been an altercation between him and "two women" who he identified as 53-year-old Lydia Leakey and her 14-year-old daughter Norma. "They're in there," he said, pointing towards the trees. "Put me in a car and I'll take you there."

A short while later, officers were following Goozee along a muddy path through the forest. Mrs. Leakey and her daughter were found in a clearing, where a steel kettle still bubbled away on a small fire. A quick examination confirmed that both women were dead. Mrs. Leaky had apparently been bludgeoned as well as stabbed while Norma had suffered a single knife wound to the chest. The bodies were removed for autopsy to Southampton mortuary.

Goozee, meanwhile, had been taken to Royal South Hants Hospital, where he remained under police guard. His stomach wound turned out to be superficial and, according to doctors, probably self-inflicted. He was soon well enough to give a statement to police and seemed more than willing to do so. In fact, it took very little coaxing before he was sharing the intimate details of a sordid tale.

According to Goozee, he'd first met Lydia Leakey when he moved into her house at 5 Alexandra Road, Parkstone, as a lodger. That was in January 1955. Within weeks of his arrival, the landlady had confided in him that she was lonely and that her husband treated her like a "beast." Thomas Leakey had lost a leg in World War II and was a moody man who slept in a separate bedroom to his wife and seemed barely to acknowledge her existence. Soon Goozee had taken up the slack, and he and Mrs. Leakey, 20 years his senior, had become lovers.

Thomas Leakey was apparently oblivious to his wife's nightly liaisons with the lodger. Not so the couple's 14-year-old daughter. One night she walked in on them and caught her mother and Goozee in the act. Then, according to Goozee, the teenager demanded a piece of the action in exchange for her silence.

And so, Goozee became the lover of both his middle-aged landlady and her teenaged daughter, a situation that continued for 18 months until Thomas Leakey eventually found out that Goozee was sleeping with his wife. The disabled war veteran then packed up his things and left. But he was back within days, demanding that Goozee move out instead.

According to Goozee, he was quite happy to escape the "unhealthy situation." But Lydia Leakey was not prepared to let go of their affair that easily. She tracked him to his new digs in Sunnyhill Road, Parkstone and pressured him to continue the relationship. Her trump card was Norma. Unless Goozee did as she asked, she said, she would take Norma to the police station and lodge a complaint of statutory rape. Left with no option, Goozee agreed.

And so to June 17, 1956, the day that Goozee drove Lydia Leakey and her daughter to a picnic at Bignell Wood in his Wolseley, a car that Mrs. Leakey had bought for him. Goozee was less forthcoming about the events of that tragic day, skimping on the details and contradicting himself several times. And the story that he did tell was difficult to swallow. He said that on arrival at the picnic spot, he had chopped some wood with an axe he'd brought along for that purpose. He had then started a fire and put a kettle on to make tea. In the meantime, Lydia had encouraged Norma to go and pick some bluebells.

Once he and Lydia were alone, she had started "pouring her heart out" about how unhappy she was without him. In the midst of this, Norma had returned and, according to Goozee, she "got all hysterical." A fight then broke out between mother and daughter, during which Norma was stabbed. Goozee had tried to separate them, but during the resulting fracas, both women were killed.

It was a quite ridiculous story and, in any case, one that was not supported by the evidence. The autopsy results were in, and they confirmed that Lydia Leakey had died from a severe skull fracture (probably caused by the ax) and from blood loss caused by her numerous stab wounds. That did not sound like a woman who had been killed accidentally. Norma had died of a single knife wound that had penetrated her heart. She had also been sexually assaulted, and that prompted detectives to construct a different narrative to the one offered by Goozee. They believed that Goozee had attacked the girl and that her mother had been killed while trying to protect her.

Albert Goozee was initially charged with sexual assault, with murder charges appended to the docket two days later. He was brought to trial in Winchester, Hampshire in early December 1956. There, a jury of seven men and five women rejected his bizarre story of accidental death resulting from a fight between mother and daughter over his affections. Goozee was found guilty and sentenced to death by hanging.

But Albert Goozee would not keep his date with the hangman. Four days before his scheduled execution, the Home Secretary intervened and commuted his sentence to life in prison. Goozee was transferred to Broadmoor, a secure psychiatric hospital where he would remain until he was paroled in 1971.

Goozee was now 48 years old and had served a mere 15 years for the brutal double homicide. But neither his narrow escape from the hangman nor his years at Broadmoor appeared to have taught him anything. In 1973, he was back in prison on a charge of theft; two years later, he was locked up again, this time for threatening a police officer with an iron bar; in 1982, he attacked a neighbor with a Stanley knife and was sentenced to 18 months. The court also revoked his parole meaning, that he would have to serve the rest of his life term.

By 1993, Albert Goozee was 70 years old and had served 26 years for his original murder charge. He was also a model prisoner who seemed to relish his role as an unofficial counselor to young inmates. The authorities must have anticipated no further trouble from him when they released him again in December of that year. They should have known better.

On Christmas Day 1995, 71-year-old Albert Goozee lured two girls, aged 12 and 13, into his house in Chatham, Kent. There, he plied them with alcohol and then indecently assaulted them. The girls later reported the attack to ChildLine, a telephone counseling service for children, resulting in Goozee's arrest. The geriatric pedophile was sentenced to six years in prison.

In 2009, a terminally-ill Albert Goozee was released from prison on compassionate grounds. He took up residence at Cedar Court nursing home for the aged in Leicestershire. He died there on November 25, 2009, after refusing all food and medication.

The Preacher's Wife

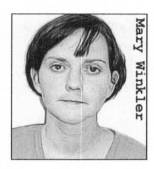

At around 6:15 on the morning of March 22, 2006, Mary Winkler was roused from sleep by the drone of her alarm clock. The petite, dark-haired woman hit the snooze button, then slid out of bed, careful not to wake her husband, Matthew, lying beside her. On naked feet, she padded across the room and opened the closet door, parting the hanging clothes to reveal the upright case that held Matthew's 12-gauge shotgun. Carefully undoing the clips, she removed the weapon. Then she carried it awkwardly back to the bed and aligned the barrel with her husband's back. Moments later, a loud boom shattered the silence of the suburban home. Matthew Winkler, the 31-year-old pastor of the Church of Christ in Selmer, Tennessee, was hit by a hail of 77 shotgun pellets that shattered his spine and lacerated his organs. Despite these massive injuries, he did not die immediately. He still found the strength to turn to his wife and utter a single word, "Why?"

"I told him that I was sorry and that I loved him," Mary would later testify. "Then I dabbed the blood from his mouth with a bed sheet and ran from the room."

The couple's three daughters had been woken by the roar of the shotgun. Mary quickly hustled them into their clothes and loaded them into her car. Minutes later, they were driving south, fleeing the jurisdiction. They spent that night at a Fairfield Inn in Jackson, Mississippi, driving on the next morning to Orange Beach, Alabama, a popular resort town on the Gulf of Mexico. There, Mary took her children to play on the beach while she contemplated what she had done. "Daddy's in the hospital," she told her oldest, Patricia, when she asked. "He's going to be fine."

Except that Matthew Winkler wasn't fine. Matthew Winkler was lying on a slab in the morgue with half of his back blown away. Church members had found him that evening when they went to check on him after he failed to show up for a regular Wednesday night prayer meeting. The Tennessee authorities then issued an Amber Alert for the three girls. It was through that alert that Mary was tracked down, after an Orange Beach patrolman recognized her daughters. While officers cared for the children – Patricia, 8; Allie, 6, and Brianna, 1 – Mary was taken into an interrogation room where she immediately confessed to shooting her husband. According to her, she'd done it because of the years of abuse she'd suffered. "I guess my ugly came out," she said. "I loved him dearly, but gosh, he just nailed me in the ground."

Mary made no objection to being returned to Tennessee, where prosecutors were already preparing a charge of first-degree murder. By now, she'd acquired a couple of high-powered Memphis lawyers, Steve Farese and Leslie Ballin. And already their approach to the case was clear. They were going to portray their client as a victim of spousal abuse, a battered woman who had fought back. What friends, family, and members of Matthew Winkler's congregation couldn't figure out, was: How had it come to this? The Winklers had always seemed like the perfect, happy family.

Mary Winkler was born Mary Carol Freeman in 1974 in Knoxville, Tennessee. Her mother was a teacher, her father a real estate investor, who bought dilapidated houses, renovated them and flipped them for a profit. There was one other child, a younger daughter named Patricia, who was a quadriplegic and died after suffering a seizure when Mary was eight. Soon after, the Freemans adopted five siblings, two boys and three girls. The family was religious, attending the Laurel Church of Christ in Knoxville where Mary's father, Clark, served as a deacon.

Mary was a bright and intelligent girl who excelled at school and maintained a heavy extracurricular schedule that included Spanish club, a Bible group, tennis, and Future Teachers of America. She graduated in 1992 from South-Doyle High School, and thereafter attended Nashville's David Lipscomb University. The following year, she transferred to Freed-Hardeman University, a Church of Christ affiliate in Henderson, Tennessee. It was there that she met Matthew Winkler.

Matthew came from a long line of preachers. His paternal grandfather, Wendell Winkler, had been a fire-and-brimstone evangelist who preached across the southeast for more than half a century. His father, Dan, had followed in Wendell's footsteps, serving as a minister of the Church of Christ and as a religious studies professor at Freed-Hardeman. There was never any doubt that Matthew would take a similar path. After graduating from Austin High School in Decatur, Alabama, he enrolled as a Bible study student at Freed-Hardeman.

Tall and handsome, a star athlete with an "infectious smile," Matthew attracted plenty of admiring glances from the opposite sex. But from the time he first laid eyes on Mary Winkler, there was only one woman for him. The couple married in Knoxville in 1996. Thereafter, both returned to their studies at Freed-Hardeman. But those studies had to be put on hold in 1997 when Mary fell pregnant. They then moved to Nashville where Matthew completed his Bible study degree while working as a youth minister at the Bellevue Church of Christ congregation. Daughter Patricia was born in October 1997, followed three years later by Mary Alice (Allie), and in March 2005 by their youngest daughter, Briana.

By now, Matthew was serving as the pulpit preacher at Fourth Street Church of Christ in Selmer, Tennessee. Selmer is a tiny community of just 4,500 inhabitants, yet it boasts over 30 churches. As the locals are also fond of pointing out, there are just three taverns in the town. Needless to say, religious faith is fervent. Some observers believe that this near-fanatical belief played a key role in the murder of Matthew Winkler.

That is because the Church of Christ favors a literal reading of the Bible. Male dominance is deeply ingrained in its doctrine, and women are expected to be subservient to their husbands. Did Mary Winkler have a problem living by that misogynistic creed? Not according to members of her husband's congregation, who swore that the couple had a harmonious marriage and that they "lived and breathed the Bible." Matthew was a beloved preacher, Mary a supportive and well-liked partner in his work. They were "good Christian people."

In August 2006, after five months behind bars, Mary Winkler was released on $750,000 bail, posted by her father. With her children (at that time) in the custody of their paternal grandparents, Mary moved to live with a friend, Kathy Thomsen, in McMinnville, Tennessee. Soon after, her attorneys, Farese and Ballin, launched a major media initiative to press the abused spouse narrative they intended pursuing at trial. It started with an article in the November 2006 issue of Glamour magazine. In it, friends and family offered testimony to Mary's saintly nature while depicting Matthew as controlling, abusive, and obsessed with money. The article was accompanied by several pictures of a demure and pensive Mary.

That theme was continued when Mary's lawyers appeared on ABC's "Good Morning America" and accused Matthew of verbal, mental, physical, and sexual abuse. It was much the same argument that they would present at trial. For now, they were making their case in the court of public opinion, and it appeared to be working. Only once did Mary's pious persona slip. On New Year's Eve 2006, someone filmed her on his cellphone, smoking and drinking at a McMinnville bar. The footage would be aired on local TV.

And so to the trial. In the run-up to the proceedings, prosecutors had approached Farese and Ballin several times, trying to negotiate a plea deal. First they'd offered 35 years, then 20, then 15. Each of these offers had been turned down. Mary's defense team was convinced that its "abused spouse narrative" would succeed. Their chances were significantly boosted by the demographics of the jury – ten women and two men.

The key evidence in the case was always going to come down to the testimony of Mary Winkler. Other witnesses – including Mary's father and two of her friends – had already laid the groundwork by the time she took the stand. They had told the court that she often hid facial bruises behind make-up; that she appeared cowered by her husband; that they had witnessed Matthew's temper first hand. But it was Mary that the court wanted to hear it from, and she didn't disappoint. She revealed that her husband forced her to engage in oral and anal sex, which she viewed as unnatural. He also made her dress up in "slutty" outfits, including an Afro wig, miniskirts and stiletto heels. Additionally, he insisted that she watch internet porn with him before they made love.

Aside from his sexual peccadillos, Matthew was physically and verbally abusive. He constantly belittled her, criticizing the way she walked, the way she sat, the way she chewed her food. He also kicked and beat her, on more than one occasion leaving her with black eyes, as described by earlier witnesses.

Farese and Ballin weren't stopping at creating justification for the shooting, though. They also introduced a commonly presented defense in gunshot cases - their client hadn't meant to kill, the gun had discharged accidentally. As to why she'd been holding the shotgun in the first place, they said she was traumatized by the ongoing abuse and that the final trigger had come the previous evening when she and Matthew had argued over money.

Raising the money issue was a clever ploy by the defense. In one fell swoop, Farese and Ballin had stolen the prosecution's thunder. The state had intended introducing the couple's financial problems as the real motive for murder, especially as many of those problems stemmed from Mary's carelessness. She had been caught in an online check-kiting scheme (commonly known as the "Nigerian scam") and had lost $17,000, money that the cash-strapped couple could hardly afford.

That had been the catalyst for the final argument and had resulted in Mary standing over her husband with the shotgun. When the gun fired "accidentally," she'd panicked and fled. It wasn't murder. It was an accident born out of years of trauma.

The Winkler trial would continue for three weeks before jurors retired to consider their verdict. After eight hours, they were back with their decision. It wasn't an acquittal, but it was the next best thing for the accused. Mary was found not guilty of murder but guilty of voluntary manslaughter. The maximum sentence she could receive was six years.

Judge McCraw came up with a somewhat lighter sentence than that – 7 months, less 143 days already served while awaiting trial, meant that Mary would spend only 67 more days behind bars. The judge further ordered that 60 of those days should be spent under evaluation at the Western State Mental Health Facility in Bolivar, Tennessee. Mary Winkler thus had just one week of prison time left to serve. It was a stunning victory for the defense.

Was justice served in the Winkler case? That depends who you ask. Jury foreman Bill Berry, one of only two male jurors, thought not. In an interview given after the trial, he called the make-up of the panel "unfair" and "unbalanced" and said that the jury had leaned heavily in favor of Mary Winkler due to the "ten ladies." They had wanted to acquit, he said, but he and the other male juror had dug their heels in. The voluntary manslaughter verdict had been a compromise.

Matthew Winkler's parents were also unhappy, not just for the verdict but for the way in which their son's reputation had been dragged through the mud. They would later file a $2 million wrongful death suit against Mary and fight her for custody of her daughters. They lost on both counts.

As for Mary, she felt that it was a hollow victory. She would serve just 210 days for shot-gunning her husband to death, but she had lost the man she loved and her children had lost their father. She would also have to live with the guilt of what she'd done for the rest of her days. "There were good and bad times in our marriage," she said. "I wish I could have the good Matthew, and we could live together forever."

The Town That Dreaded Sundown

Texarkana is unique city, or rather a unique conglomeration of cities, since the metropolitan area comprises both Texarkana, Texas, and Texarkana, Arkansas. Straddling the border of the states from which it takes its name, the metropolis rose up around a railroad junction, growing rapidly. By the mid-forties, it had reached a population of around 44,000. This is the era in which our story takes place.

It started on the night of Friday, February 22, 1946. Jimmy Hollis had taken his girlfriend Mary Jeanne Larey to a movie that night and had thereafter driven his father's Plymouth to a secluded stretch of Richmond Road, a popular "lovers' lane" on the outskirts of town. Hollis cut the engine of the car at 11:45 and then cuddled up in the front seat with Mary Jeanne. They'd barely gotten comfortable when a flashlight was shone through the driver's window, blinding Hollis. He at first thought that it might be a policeman out on patrol. Realizing that it wasn't, he told the man holding the light: "Fellow, you've got me mixed up with someone else. You've got the wrong man." The stranger then ordered him from the car, assuring Hollis that he would not be hurt as long as he did as he was told. Hollis then exited the vehicle, leaving his girlfriend inside.

With the light still shining in his eyes, Hollis could not make out the man's features. He could, however, hear him well enough. What the man was telling him to do was to remove his "britches." Hollis initially refused, only complying after the man threatened to kill him. "He sounded crazy," Hollis would later tell the police. Crazy enough not to be messed with. Hollis did as he was told.

But that didn't save him from the wrath of his assailant. He'd barely stepped out his trousers when something came crashing down hard onto his skull. Then he was hit again, and again, spilling him to the dusty earth.

To Mary Jeanne Larey, watching panic-stricken from the car, the blows sounded so loud that she thought they were gunshots. With Hollis dazed on the ground, the assailant continued his attack, kicking and stomping until his victim eventually lay still. Then he turned his attention to the Plymouth and beckoned Mary Jeanne with a hand gesture. She could see now that he was wearing a crude mask, a feedbag with holes cut for the eyes and mouth. She could also see that he was holding a gun.

Traumatized by what she'd seen, terrified at what might happen to her, Mary Jeanne got out of the car. Seeking to buy some time, she told the assailant that neither she nor Hollis had any money. That just seemed to infuriate him. "Liar!" he screamed and demanded her purse. It was at that moment that Mary Jeanne's survival instinct kicked in. She suddenly sprinted for cover, taking off into the darkness. However, the high heels she was wearing hampered her flight. Soon she heard the man blundering after her, repeatedly shouting "Liar!" as he ran. Moments later, he crashed into her, tackling her to the ground. Then he was fumbling with her clothes, touching her where she had never been touched before. Exhausted, pinned to the ground by her much stronger attacker, there was nothing she could do about it.

Mary Jeanne Larey would later be reluctant to speak about the sexual assault she endured. She would eventually admit that her attacker had violated her with the barrel of his gun. Who knows what other indignities might have been forced upon her had the attacker not been frightened off by a passing car. Then Mary Jeanne managed to stagger to the road and flag down a motorist. Both she and Jimmy Hollis would survive the ordeal. They were the lucky ones.

In the early morning hours of March 24, one month after the attack on Hollis and Larey, a trucker was driving his vehicle along Highway 67 when he spotted a 1941 Oldsmobile parked in a grove of trees just off Robinson Road. There was a man asleep behind the wheel, which the truck driver thought unsafe, given the earlier attacks in the area. He decided to stop and wake the man and point him in the direction of a nearby motel.

But the Olds driver was beyond waking. He was dead, a bullet hole perforating his forehead. Horrified, the trucker drove immediately to alert the police. They arrived to find that the dead driver was only half of the story. There was another body in the car, a young woman lying face down on the back seat. The victims would later be identified as 29-year-old Richard Griffin and his 17-year-old girlfriend, Polly Ann Moore. Ballistics would prove that they had both been shot with a .32-caliber Colt pistol. Robbery was thought to be the likely motive for the killing, although the police erred in ignoring other possibilities. There was evidence, for example, that the female victim had been shot to death while lying on a blanket in front of the car. That suggested a sexual motive, but no tests were done to confirm this.

Of greater concern to the police was that the two attacks might be connected. Was there a killer out there preying on couples parked in lovers' lanes? The similarities between the crimes certainly seemed to suggest so, and the Bowie County Sheriff's Department, therefore, decided to call in extra help, including from the famed Texas Rangers. The man assigned to lead the Ranger contingent was Captain Manuel "Lone Wolf" Gonzaullas, a larger-than-life character who looked like a throwback to the Old West. Gonzaullas was soon parading around town in his signature white ten-gallon hat, pearl-handled revolvers slung low around his waist. During his first few days in Texarkana, he gave a number of radio and newspaper interviews in which he assured the locals that the killer would soon be in handcuffs. Those promises, unfortunately, turned out to be wide of the mark.

Betty Jo Booker was a talented young musician. At the age of just 15, she was a saxophonist with the popular local band, Jerry Atkins and his Rhythmaires. On the evening of Saturday, April 13, the Rhythmaires played a gig at the VFW Club on Oak Street, finishing their last set just after 1 a.m. Normally, Atkins would drive his young sax player home after the gig, but on this night Betty Jo told him not to bother. She would be attending a slumber party nearby and was getting a ride with Paul Martin, a childhood friend who was visiting from Kilgore, Texas. Martin looked like a nice enough young man, and so Atkins agreed. Later he'd have cause to regret that decision.

At around 6:30 on the morning of April 14, a man named Weaver was driving his family out of Texarkana, on route to Prescott, Arkansas, when he spotted a 1946 Ford Coupe, apparently abandoned near the entrance to Spring Lake Park. Weaver stopped off at the next residence along the road and called the police. Soon the area was flooded with officers, and it did not take long before they discovered Paul Martin's body, lying on its side in the vicinity of North Park Road. He had been shot four times – in the face, the neck, the abdomen, and through the hand. Defensive wounds suggested that he'd put up a fierce fight for his life.

Betty Jo Booker's body was found four hours later and two miles away. She too had been shot, one bullet entering her left cheek and another penetrating the chest cavity via the ribcage. Either would have been fatal. Evidence suggested that Betty Jo had been raped, and ballistics would later confirm the worst fears of law officers. The bullets had been fired from the same weapon that had killed Jimmy Hollis and Mary Jeanne Larey. Although the term was not yet in common usage, Texarkana had a serial killer on its streets.

And the killer (labeled "The Phantom" by the media) was sparking a citywide panic. By night, the streets resembled those of a ghost town with terrified citizens crouched behind locked doors with fully loaded weapons. There was a run on deadbolts and alarm systems. Those who couldn't afford alarms constructed their own, out of tin cans, kitchen utensils and yarn. The only exceptions to this siege mentality were the teenaged gangs who took to the streets at night to "hunt" the Phantom. Some even foolhardily parked in cars on quiet streets, hoping to lure the killer. The police had a full-time job trying to control these youthful vigilantes. That, perhaps, gave the killer an opportunity to strike again.

Virgil and Katy Starks lived in a modest ranch-style house on 500 acres in Miller County, Arkansas, some 12 miles from Texarkana. The middle-aged couple would obviously have been aware of the Phantom, but they would not have considered themselves potential victims. The killer, after all, preyed on couple's 'parking' in cars. His hunting ground was also closer to the city limits. Virgil and Katy probably thought that they were safe. They were wrong in that assumption.

On the evening of May 3, Virgil was in the lounge, a heating pad
pressed to his aching back while he relaxed in his favorite easy chair.
He had the radio on, country music playing in the background while he
scanned the evening edition of the *Texarkana Daily News*.

Katy was in the bedroom flipping through a magazine when she heard
glass breaking. That was followed by the distinct report of a gunshot,
which sent Katy rushing to the lounge. There, she saw Virgil, still
sitting in his chair with blood flowing from a head wound and
spattering the newspaper that was still open in his lap. Acting more on
instinct than conscious thought, Katy ran immediately for the wall-
crank telephone to call the police. That was when two more shots rang
out, both of them hitting her in the head.

Katy immediately collapsed to the floor, badly injured. One of the
bullets had entered her right cheek, traveling on a trajectory that
punched it through her skull behind the left ear. The second had struck
her in the lower jaw, shattering her teeth. Yet despite her injuries, Katy
was determined to live. She crawled on her belly towards the back
door, only to find that the killer was trying to force his way in,
growling and cussing like a rabid beast. Those inhuman cries provided
Katy with all the motivation she needed. Summoning strength from
her fear, she pulled herself to her feet and staggered through the house
towards the front door, exiting that way and making her way across the
road to her sister's house. Finding no one home, she lurched towards
the home of her neighbors, the Praters, who drove her to the nearby
Michael Meagher Hospital. Amazingly, Katy remained conscious
throughout this entire episode. She had lost a lot of blood and suffered
horrendous facial injuries, but neither of the bullets had penetrated her
brain.

Virgil Starks was not so lucky. Officers who arrived at the crime scene found him still seated in his easy chair, which was now smoldering from the heat pack. It would be determined that the killer had fired through the lounge window, hitting him in the head and killing him instantly.

The scene presented the police with three workable clues. The first was the type of weapon used, a .22 rifle rather than the .23 semi-automatic used in the other Phantom killings (this would lead some investigators to decide that the Starks attack was committed by a different perpetrator). The second was the muddy footprints left all over the house by the killer. The third was a flashlight found under a hedge near the front door.

But despite these clues the police would make scant progress in tracking down the Phantom. Part of the problem was that they were suddenly inundated with tip-offs, some in response to a reward offered for information, some offered vindictively as a way of settling petty disputes. A long list of suspects was generated, ranging from an escaped German POW to a gay student at the University of Arkansas. The most likely candidate appeared to be a career criminal named Youell Swinney, whose own wife named him as the Phantom before withdrawing her statement and stating that she would refuse to testify against her husband should the matter ever come to trial. It never did, although Swinney remains the favored suspect of most scholars of the case.

That was perhaps the death knell of the investigation. Over time, with no further attacks or murders, things slowly got back to normal in Texarkana. Where once there'd been officers from four jurisdictions

patrolling the streets, patrols were scaled back to pre-crisis levels;
where once the city's businesses had shuttered their doors after dark,
now the bars and clubs started doing steady trade again. One regular
feature of Texarkana nightlife was gone forever, though. After the
death of Betty Jo Booker, Jerry Atkins decided to disband the
Rhythmaires. They'd never play another note.

The Texarkana Moonlight Murders remain unsolved to this day, one of
the great mysteries of American crime. There have been several books
on the case, both biographical and fictional. The case also inspired a
1976 movie (remade in 2014) called *The Town That Dreaded
Sundown*, from which this chapter takes its name.

For more True Crime books by Robert Keller

please visit:

http://bit.ly/kellerbooks

Made in the USA
Coppell, TX
02 July 2021

58495356R00083